The Science of Yoga - Impact of Mudras, Bandhas, and Chakras

Prof. Bharat Raj Singh
Satish Kumar Singh
Prof. Ajay Kumar Singh

The Science of Yoga – Impact of Mudras, Bandhas, and Chakras:

Health Benefits through Spiritual Method

Vedic Science Centre, Lucknow

The Science of Yoga – Impact of Mudras, Bandhas, and Chakras: Health Benefits through Spiritual Method
Published: Oct 2023
Edition: First
ISBN: 978-1-304-99767-8

Description:

Yoga Science is an ancient Indian discipline that traces its roots back five thousand years to the Vedas, a collection of texts authored by Vedvyas during the Treta Yuga. The essence of Yoga is elucidated within these sacred scriptures, which form part of the Sanatana Dharma and encompass the 4 Vedas, 18 Puranas, and 108 Upanishads. Within the Vedic teachings, the definition of Yoga is expounded. Furthermore, the Yoga Sutras of Maharishi Patanjali, known as Raja Yoga or Ashtanga Yoga, outline the principles of leading a righteous life. These sutras encompass eight limbs, namely: (i) Yama, (ii) Niyama, (iii) Asana, (iv) Pranayama, (v) Pratyahara, (vi) Dharana, (vii) Meditation, and (viii) Samadhi. The practice of these eight limbs enables the awakening of mudras, bandhas, and chakras within the physical body, leading to various health benefits. The book explains in a simplified manner how one can cultivate virtuous living by channeling vital energy through the use of mudras, bandhas, and kriyas from the Muladhara Chakra to the Sahasrara Chakra.

Author:

Dr. Bharat Raj Singh, Director General & Incharge
Vedic Science Center, School of Management Sciences,
(Affiliated to Abdul Kalam Technical University)
19th Km, Lucknow-Sultanpur Road, Kasimpur Biruha, Lucknow - 226501, India.

Website: www.smslucknow.ac.in **E-mail:** brsingh@smslucknow.ac.in

Fixed Price and License:

INR ₹1100, approx. (US$13.50)

Publisher:

lulu Lulu Press Inc.
627, Davis Drive, Suite 300, Morrisville, NC 27560, USA
www.Lulu.com; Copyright © 2022 Lulu.com

Dedicated

(**Born:** 1940 - **Death**: 2023)

This book is dedicated to the memory of Late Shri Ramayan Singh, whose noble spirit now resides in the vast cosmos. He consistently provided unwavering support to the Vedic Science Centre, encouraging us to explore the depths of our ancient Vedic Scripture and embrace the path of critical thinking.

His genuine inspiration and unwavering enthusiasm propelled me to embark on an extensive research journey, delving into the profound benefits of spirituality and uncovering the scientific methodologies of yoga for the betterment of society. As a result, I authored an English version book on the subject titled: "*The Science of Yoga - Impact of Mudras, Bandhas, and Chakras,*" which has been successfully published.

Message

Anandiben Patel
Governor, Uttar Pradesh

सत्यमेव जयते

Raj Bhavan
Lucknow - 226 027

27 October, 2023

I am delighted to learn that a book titled: **'The Yoga Science - Impact of Mudras, Bandhas and Chakras - Health Benefits through Spiritual Method'** is being published by the Vedic Science Center, School of Management Sciences, Lucknow.

Impact of Yoga holds immense significance in our contemporary world. As we navigate the demands of modern life, the ancient wisdom encapsulated within the practices of mudras, bandhas and chakras takes on new relevance. I believe this publication will be a guiding light for those seeking a deeper understanding of the profound connection between science and spirituality.

I extend my heartfelt congratulations and best wishes for the successful publication of the book. May it serve as a source of profound knowledge and well-being for its readers.

Anandi Patel

(Anandiben Patel)

Telephone : 0522-2236497 Fax : 0522-2239488 Email : hgovup@gov.in Website : www.upgovernor.gov.in

Preface

Yoga Science is an ancient Indian knowledge system that dates back five thousand years and finds its roots in the Vedas authored by Vedvyas during the Treta Yuga. The Sanatan Dharma encompasses four (4) Vedas, eighteen (18) Puranas, and one hundred and eight (108) Upanishads, where the definition of Yoga is mentioned. The Yoga Sutras of Maharishi Patanjali, known as Raja Yoga or Ashtanga Yoga, provide guidance on leading a balanced life. These teachings encompass eight components: Yama, Niyama, Asana, Pranayama, Pratyahara, Dharana, Meditation, and Samadhi. By delving into the knowledge of ancient yoga, we can uncover the profound yet simple principles of Yama and Niyama, which serve as the foundation for a joyful and healthy life. For instance, the principle of "Santosh" emphasizes the importance of contentment, while "Aparigraha" aids in overcoming anxiety and tension caused by greed and attachment. The "Sauch" principle focuses on mental and physical purification, particularly beneficial in times of concern about infectious diseases. Embracing the Yamas and Niyamas of Yoga can assist in adopting a nutritious diet and leading a healthy lifestyle, leading to reduced stress and anxiety.

In India, the tradition of devoutly worshiping and surrendering oneself to God has persisted from ancient mythology to the present day, often accompanied by the use of herbal remedies to treat ailments, including incurable diseases. It is worth examining whether this practice solely provides mental satisfaction or if it possesses a scientific foundation. Our books and historical records discuss the integration of both "medicine and spirituality" for the treatment of diseases, prompting the need for in-depth exploration and study.

The human body is composed of five elemental components: earth, water, fire, air, and sky. Within the body, there exist five layers known as sheaths or koshas: Annamaya Kosha (physical sheath), Pranamaya Kosha (vital energy sheath), Manomaya Kosha (mental sheath), Vijnanamaya Kosha (intellectual sheath), and Anandamaya Kosha (bliss sheath). The overall well-being of the body, mind, and soul depends on maintaining a healthy balance of these elements or cells. Imbalances or ailments in these aspects can lead to physical and mental illnesses. Fortunately, hand postures, known as mudras, can be practiced to restore balance and promote health.

The book "*The Science of Yoga - Impact of Mudras, Bandhas, and Chakras,*" guides readers on how to channel energy from the Muladhar Chakra to the Sahasrar Chakra, thereby infusing vitality into the physical body and leading a virtuous life. The book also provides instructions on awakening the chakras through the practice of mudras and bandhas. Before engaging in these practices, it is essential to acquire knowledge about the Science behind yoga and understand how to attain health benefits by awakening mudras, bandhas, and chakras within the physical body using Yoga techniques. By embracing the principles of Puranic Yoga Science presented in this book, individuals can alleviate ailments caused by blocked chakras and cultivate a purposeful life focused on serving others.

The book is structured into eight chapters, each offering valuable insights on various aspects of Yoga:

1. Introduction to Yoga Science and its practices
2. The significance of prayer, reverence, and a smiling disposition

3. Understanding Yoga Mudras and its importance
4. Exploring specific Mudras and Mahamudra Asanas
5. Types and benefits of Yoga bandhas
6. The importance of Chakras within the body
7. Techniques for attaining bodily happiness
8. The practice of Yoga and its associated benefits

The book "*The Science of Yoga - Impact of Mudras, Bandhas, and Chakras,*" has been carefully organized into eight chapters, offering a comprehensive and practical approach to utilizing body postures, bandhas, and chakras for the alleviation of incurable diseases. It is our sincere hope that readers will find great value and benefits through the knowledge presented in this book.

Furthermore, we have included insightful discussions with experienced yoga practitioners, encompassing topics such as yoga philosophy, superbrain yoga, meditation, and pranic energy. These additional practices are intended to enhance the reader's understanding and provide them with diverse tools for self-improvement. We eagerly anticipate receiving feedback from readers about their personal experiences with the book. By sharing these experiences and spreading the knowledge to as many individuals as possible, we can collectively benefit and inspire others. Your valuable suggestions are always welcome, as they contribute to the continual refinement and meaningfulness of this book.

Sincerely,

Prof. Bharat Raj Singh
Satish Kumar Singh
Prof. Ajay Kumar Singh

Acknowledgement

Over 500 articles published in daily newspapers/magazines since April 2015 by Vedic Science Center, Lucknow, unveiling the benefits of ancient mythological texts for Society's well-being. In this sequence, on the demand of the public and on the suggestion of the members and friends of the Vedic Science Center, I have got the opportunity to write a book on the title "The Science of Yoga – Impact of Mudras, Bandhas, and Chakras". Along with mythological texts, spiritual thinkers, experimental experiences of some foreign institutions and spiritual thinking, I have mentioned the simple methods of its implementation and how its benefits reach the public, in a sequential form; Which is divided into 08-chapters, in which mainly to get information about yoga-science before practicing and how to get health benefits by awakening hand postures, bands and chakras in the physical body through yoga method, simple and The active method is described in detail. I hope readers will take advantage of this and also send their suggestions.

First and foremost, we extend our deepest gratitude to the esteemed Governor of Uttar Pradesh, Mrs. Anandiben Patel, who presides over one of the largest states of our nation. This expression of thanks is conveyed not only on my behalf but also on behalf of all members of the Vedic Science Center, the college administration, including CEO, Shri Sharad Singh and the Vice-Chancellor of Abdul Kalam Technical University, Prof. JP Pandey. Our center will forever remain indebted to her, as her blessings will serve as the guiding force in our endeavor to alleviate incurable physical ailments through the awakening of mudras, bandhas, and chakras. It is hoped that the readers will definitely take advantage of how to make the physical body healthy and lead a virtuous life by means of actions from Muladhar Chakra to Sahasrar Chakra, as mentioned in the book "The Science of Yoga – Impact of Mudras, Bandhas, and Chakras".

Shri Satish Kumar Singh, the founder and chairman of the School of Management Sciences in Lucknow, and a trailblazer in the spiritual domain, along with Prof. Ajay Kumar Singh, a dedicated yoga practitioner and healer, are not only enriching their own understanding but also disseminating knowledge to the wider community through their daily engagement in yoga practices. I extend my heartfelt appreciation to both of them for their invaluable contributions as co-authors, which have breathed life into this book through their significant insights and suggestions.

Here the author would like to thank all the respected members of the Vedic Science Center, who have given their suggestions from time to time, due to which this mythology of India is being propagated as a ritual to the teachers and students. In this sequence, all those people, in particular; Dr. Manoj Kumar Mehrotra, Director, School of Management Sciences, Lucknow; Associate Director, Dr. Dharmendra Singh; Dean-Student Welfare, Dr. P.K. Singh, etc., who have always been helpful in shaping this book and the publishers, Lulu Press Incl., USA and others who have directly or indirectly contributed to this book, express their heartfelt thanks and appreciation.

The author wishes to extend heartfelt gratitude to his wife, Mrs. Malti Singh, and his children - Nidhi and Rahul Singh, Saurabh and Deepika Singh, Gaurav Singh - as well as his grandchildren - Navaditya, Nandika, Jayani, and Jaitra, and others who have consistently contributed to this work for the betterment of the public. Their unwavering support and encouragement have played a pivotal role in shaping the book "The Science of Yoga – Impact of Mudras, Bandhas, and Chakras."

Finally, the authors would like to express their sincere thanks to Mr. Sharad Singh, Secretary and Chief Executive Officer at the School of Management Sciences, Lucknow, for his continuous encouragement and valuable suggestions throughout the process.

Prof. Bharat Raj Singh,
Director General (Technical),
School of Management Sciences and
Chairman, Vedic Science Center,
Lucknow.

Contents

Summary

Yoga Science, an age-old tradition with a history of over five thousand years, finds its origins in the Vedas, meticulously composed by Vedvyas during the Treta Yuga. At the core of this profound discipline lies Sanatan Dharma, which encompasses four Vedas, eighteen Puranas, and a hundred and eight Upanishads. It's within these sacred texts that the very essence of Yoga's definition is enshrined.

Subsequently, the science of righteous living was distilled from the profound teachings within the Yoga Sutras of Maharishi Patanjali. This collection, often referred to as Raja Yoga or Ashtanga Yoga, represents a comprehensive system that integrates all facets of Yoga into eight fundamental components: Yama, Niyama, Asana, Pranayama, Pratyahara, Dharana, Meditation, and Samadhi. These components, in turn, possess their own intricate sub-elements.

Following this sequence, delving into the ancient wisdom of Yoga not only acquaints us with its foundational principles (yamas and niyamas), but also illuminates a path towards a joyful and healthful existence. For instance, the principle of 'Santosh' encourages us to embrace contentment as a vital aspect of life. 'Aparigraha', another principle, guides us towards liberation from the turmoil of greed and attachment, fostering tranquility and alleviating inner tension. The 'Sauch' principle, on the other hand, emphasizes the purification of both mind and body, fostering a state of holistic well-being, when concerns about contracting infectious diseases are paramount. Within the framework of yoga's yamas and niyamas, this principle assumes a crucial role in guiding individuals towards making informed dietary choices and adopting a health-conscious way of life. By adhering to these principles, one can pave the way to not only better nutrition but also an overall healthier lifestyle. This, in turn, becomes a potent tool in mitigating stress and anxiety, offering a substantial measure of relief. Hence, acquiring a comprehensive understanding of The Science of Yoga becomes pivotal before embarking on its practice.

In India, from ancient times till today, in the common activities of the people, along with the use of herbs to cure any illness or incurable disease, there has been a practice of worshiping God with devotion and inner heart. Is . Have we tried to understand this carefully, does it merely give satisfaction to the mind or does it have any scientific basis? , Since the discussion of adopting both 'medicine and medicine' for the treatment of any disease is found in our texts and pages of history, there seems to be an absolute need to study it in depth. In the same sequence, in this book: The Science of Yoga - Impact of Mudras, Bandha and Chakras, it has been explained about how awakening of Mudras, Bandhas and Chakras in the physical body through spiritual method provides health benefits.

When a chakra or wheel of energy becomes stuck, movement can help release the prana (energy). Yoga postures are a great way to release stale or stuck energy from the body as they invite fresh, vital energy back in through the posture and breath.

In the continuation of above, ultimately the practice of yoga leads us to a state of union, which is possible when we create a state in our body where energy flows freely from the base of the spine, the root chakra to the head and beyond that, flow can occur up to the crown chakra. When each chakra is unblocked, it rotates like a wheel, hence the word 'chakra' meaning 'wheel' in Sanskrit. This way energy can flow freely through us, so we can achieve a state of unity with the cosmic energy that flows through all living things.

This book has been divided into 8-chapters in which the effects of hand Mudras, Bandhas and Chakras of the body to stay healthy and simple and active methods (with pictures) and treatment methods to release the blocked energy in different places of the body and its details have also been given about the specific benefits of its use in various diseases.

1.0
Science of Yoga & Its Regular Practice

When we delve into the essence of the term "yoga", it primarily embodies two concepts. Firstly, it signifies the union between the Soul and the Divine, epitomizing the experience of non-duality. This culminates in a profound connection with the Supreme Father, God. As elucidated in the literal interpretation of Yoga above, it delineates the path through which the soul attains communion with the Supreme Soul. This path, in essence, can be aptly termed Yoga. It's more accurate to assert that by harmonizing the disturbances of the mind, the ultimate objective is to connect with the Supreme Soul. The process of attaining this oneness is termed Yoga. In contemporary times, the term 'yoga' has been attributed to the practice of maintaining bodily health and exercise. However, it's crucial to recognize that exercise alone doesn't encapsulate the entirety of yoga; rather, it represents just one facet or dimension of the complete yogic philosophy.

There are many spiritual ways of meeting the divine, the name of yoga has been associated with all of them.

In this way, many branches of yoga are prevalent since ancient times, some of them are as follows-

(1) Kriya Yoga, (2) Raja Yoga, (3) Hatha Yoga, (4) Japa Yoga, (5) Laya Yoga, (6) Mantra Yoga, (7) Shabda Yoga, (8) Gyaana Yoga, (9) Karma Yoga, (10) Bhakti Yoga, (11) Praan Yoga, (12) Hansa Yoga, (13) Tantra Yoga, (14) Swara Yoga, (15) Shiva Yoga, (16) Bhrigu Yoga, (17) Dhyana Yoga etc, etc...

Here partial information is being given about the most powerful method of Yoga - ***Kriya Yoga,*** which was initiated by Yogiraj Lord Shri Krishna and is still present in front of us through the tradition of Guru Shishya (Figure-1.1).

Figure 1.1: Kriya Yoga – Teacher-Student Tradition

1.1 Kriya Yoga

Kriya Yoga is also called practical and simple because the devotees can directly experience whatever subject matter is explained and taught in it. This is why Kriya Yoga is considered supreme, looking at these specialties of Kriya Yoga, we can say that it is not a miracle but a science, which is proven on the basis of science. Our sages and great yogis of India have preserved this precious heritage of Kriya Yoga even today, the importance of which is also accepted by today's scientists.

Mahavatar Baba, a timeless, historical man who was physically present through the power of Yoga for thousands of years, made the science of Kriyayoga known to the whole world through his capable disciples. Something about Mahavatar Baba and his disciples who created history and became historical men. Writing would be like showing a lamp to the sun.

Soul always tries to get rid of sorrows, that is, it has been proved that sorrow is not the soul's own nature, sorrow is not the soul's object. The soul is a pure form which continuously searches for knowledge to get relief from suffering. Knowledge is the cause of freedom from sorrows, about this we can say this, we acquire knowledge in five ways, the first knowledge is given by our parents, that is, our first gurus were our parents. Second knowledge is given by good books, that is, second Guru's books. The third knowledge is given to us by our real Guru, be it spiritual or practical. The fourth knowledge is our experience, which we keep getting everyday in the form of experience generated knowledge. The fifth knowledge we get in the state of meditation "Samadhi", in the state of Samadhi, the soul is interviewed with the divine, that is, the soul meets with the divine and when this happens then there is nothing left to know and understand- It doesn't survive because, God reveals his own form by himself, and when this happens then there is nothing left to know, because there is nothing in front of God, the father of the whole universe. We should always try to have the above five types of knowledge in our lives.

If we consider the concept of Big-Bang, then all the molecules separated from one mass and exist in the form of the present universe in their course of travel. We living beings created from these molecules have also completed their journey of gradual development till present, Charles Darwin's theory of gradual development also propounds the same. So it is confirmed that all the experiences/memories of the journey from the big bang till today are included in our brain. When a Kriya Yogi becomes conscious of these hidden memories/feelings lying in the depths of his subconscious mind by going into the state of meditation and samadhi, then nothing remains unknowable for the Yogi, the Yogi becomes familiar with the hidden secrets of this creation. He is the knower of its beginning and end, that is, his divine eyes open and he becomes trikaldarshi.

पृथ्व्याप्यतेजोऽनिलखे समुत्थिते पञ्चात्मके योगगुणे प्रवृत्ते ।
न तस्य रोगो न जरा न मृत्युः प्राप्तस्य योगाग्निमयं शरीरम्॥ १२॥

(svetasvatara upnishad)

When earth, water, light, wind and sky appear, that is, the five elements are conquered, then there is neither disease, nor old age, nor sorrow for the yogi, because he has got the body which is capable of yoga. Made of fire.

Western psychologist Sigmund Freud has said that the normal human being uses only 3 to 4 percent of his brain, the rest of the brain remains inactive in a state of dormancy, a Kriya Yogi can awaken that sleeping-inactive brain through his yoga practice. By interviewing all the pastimes of the Supreme Father God, he becomes one with the Supreme Soul.

Along with Sanatan Dharma, many other religions also accept the principle of Karma Fruit that whatever work we do, we definitely get the result of the work done. There is a reason for every work in the form of sorrow and happiness and the reason is always created in the past. Whether that past tense is of this life or of a past life - this principle is proved. We ourselves are the creators of the life we are living today, and we have created our present life at some point in the past. Sigmund Freud has expressed the idea that whatever good and bad deeds a man does It goes into his subconscious mind, that is, it gets registered and then that sanskar in the form of karma recorded in the subconscious mind controls the future life. This idea proves that we are the creators of our own future and we choose our own birth and rebirth.

It is because of the above reasons that Indian sages and great yogis have developed various methods of spiritual practice for leading a regular, restrained and spiritual life, and for self-development, which are accessible to the whole world.

1.2 Kriya Yogi

Kriya Yogi is the one who, after leading his life on the path of practice and sadhana, reaches the state of Samadhi through continuous practice and erases the impressions of good and bad karma recorded in the subconscious mind from many births and frees himself from the bondage of the results of karma. That is, it completely eliminates it. Because when there are no sanskars left, then the reason for the work is no longer left, that is, the ultimate goal of the soul is to get relief from suffering, i.e. attaining salvation and getting freedom from the world of sorrow. That is why the importance of this method of Kriya Yoga, propounded by our sages and great yogis, has also been accepted by modern scientists.

India has a glorious history full of enlightenment since ancient times. Here, on the fundamental question of life, our sages and scientists in the form of great yogis, through their penance and research, propounded such principles and placed them before the entire world community, by adopting which the entire world can benefit itself. Despite centuries of slavery, persecution and attempts to wipe it out, the whole world is looking at our heritage which is left today. The land of India has never been empty of sages, great yogis and wise men who have rejuvenated the entire human society. This land has been producing a prophet in every century, who gives the message of Amber, that is, "the great man of the era, the messenger of God" who gives divine knowledge.

यदा यदा ही धर्मस्य ग्लानिर्भवति भारत ।
अभ्युत्थसनमधर्मस्य तदात्मानं सृजाम्यहम्॥ (भगवद्गीता. 4.7)

Whenever righteousness begins to decline and unrighteousness begins to advance, then I create myself, that is, I take birth. I incarnate in different eras for the protection of the good, the destruction of the wicked and the re-establishment of religion.

Figure1.2: Kriya Yoga - Sadhana and Practice

Indian Sanatana Dharma: Based on 4-Vedas, 108-Upanishads,18-Puranas and 12-Philosophy. Many sects support only one philosophy, but the foundation stone of the land of India is based on 12-philosophies; 6-Philosophy theist and 6-Philosophy atheist. This land also adopts the extremely atheistic Charvak philosophy. Because Sanatan Dharma respects everyone by imbibing everyone's ideology.

Even after this, Sanatan Dharma says neti-neti. That is, this is not the end, there is much more left to know before this, because God is infinite. The creation created by God is also eternal.

Man is normal only until he conquers or rises above nature. Within this nature, not only those laws apply, which govern our atomic structure, but there are also such subtle laws which govern the subconscious nature which governs the visible nature. It is easy to conquer the visible world, but to conquer the inner world is called the ultimate effort. We get this ultimate effort through the meditation and practice of Kriya Yoga (Figure1.2).

As strange and special as our external world is, our inner world is equally mysterious and full of supernatural vision. To journey into this world of supernatural mystery, we need to know why we are the way we are today. What is the reason for this ? What is our ultimate goal? And five types of sorrow:

1. Avidya (No Knowledge)
2. Identity
3. Raga
4. Hatred and
5. Investment,

Figure 1.3: Kriya Yoga – Mysterious and supernatural vision

Let us make Kriya Yoga our vehicle for freedom from all the causes of suffering and take out some time from the busy schedule of our worldly life to achieve our goal, which is our ultimate aim and goal.

भोगा न भुक्ता वयमेव भुक्तास्तपो न तप्तम वयमेव तप्ताः ।
कालो न यातो वयमेव यातास्तृष्णा न जीर्णा वयमेव जीर्णाः ॥

That is, the pleasures were not enjoyed (we did not enjoy the pleasures), but we were enjoyed; I didn't do penance, I did penance; Time has not passed, but we have passed, the desire has not become old, but we ourselves have become old (Figure1.3).

1.3 Yoga science and regular practice

Knowing and applying ancient yoga knowledge, exposes us to the simple but profound yogic principles (yamas and niyamas) of Patanjali's Shashtang Yoga - Yama, Niyama, Asana, Praanyama, Pratyahara, Dharana, Dhyana, and Samadhi, which help us This can become the essence of a happy and healthy life. For example, the principle of 'Satisfaction' makes one realize the importance of being satisfied in life. 'Aparigraha' principle - helps in freeing one from anxiety, restlessness and stress caused by greed and attachment. The principle of 'Shaucha' tells about mental and physical purification. This rule especially helps you when you are worried about contracting infectious diseases. The principles and rules of yoga will help you in eating nutritious food and leading a healthy lifestyle, which will help you to overcome stress and anxiety to a great extent. Therefore, it is very important for us to get information about the science of yoga before practicing it.

1.4 Some important points

a) **How many days a week is it beneficial to do yoga:** Since yoga is a science, practicing it without understanding it can be harmful. If you do yoga even for an hour a week, it is very beneficial. The more you do this, the benefits increase. Some people suggest that one should practice for one hour at least three times a week. Even if you have a 20-minute session every day, it is quite beneficial.

b) **Is yoga effective only in flexible people:** Flexibility in the body is not an essential condition for yoga. People who do not have flexibility in their body can also do yoga. Yoga helps in gaining flexibility in their body.

c) **What is necessary to start yoga:** The most important thing for practicing yoga is preparation of body and mind. To do yoga, you can use leggings or shorts or t-shirt as a dress. Keep in mind that none of these should be too loose. There is no need to wear any special footwear for yoga.

d) **Why you should not eat food before yoga:** According to experts, to do yoga, food should be done only after three hours of eating, because yoga practice

2.0
Prayer, Faith and Smile

Prayer is the best source to be free from worries. By adopting habits like praying regularly, chanting mantras, chanting bhajans, we are filled with positive energy and these help in stabilizing the mind. It fills us with a deep faith and reverence that whatever is happening is for our good and that there is a supreme divine power that takes care of us all. Apart from this, make a conscious effort to smile as much as possible. It will automatically fill you with confidence, peace and positivity. Try using it immediately (Figure-2.1).

Many people experience many unusual things in their lifetime that cannot be verified. Often they don't even seem true. It seems that they appear from some pneumatic world or from the void. Such experiences include premonition of some event, dreams seen during sleep coming true and seeing ghosts etc. Such events are considered supernatural because they cannot be explained by known physical laws.

In his book 'Frontiers of the Mind', JB Rinn of Stanford University, who was authorised to study such unusual phenomena, has proved with dozens of examples that it is pure nonsense to deny those things which we cannot understand from known physical laws. This science is related to the study of secret powers or phenomena such as telepathy, ghosts, etc., which have not been understood till now. The laboratory at Duke conducted experiments on extrasensory perception following standard scientific procedures, the results of which were recognized throughout the world.

Following these results, in 1937, psychologists studied many paranormal phenomena and explained them. This was confirmed at a spiritual conference held in Gothenburg, the city of Wieden. In it, A. of Christian Science Review. D. Stewart said that life after death is not recognized in Christianity. Nor has life after death been denied. Yet, out of all the cases that have come under the ambit of parapsychology, most of them are from the Christian world.

Figure-2.1: Prayer – Gain Positive Energy

The word prayer is made up of 'pra' and 'artha', which means to request with full concentration. In other words, prayer means a request made with intense desire for something from God.

One thing we all see from our birth is that our parents, teachers and our friends are engaged in the development of our five senses, mind and intellect. In the present world, there is too much emphasis on things related to the five senses, mind, and intellect like external beauty, our salary, our circle of friends, etc. Most of us are not told at any stage of life that the purpose of our life is to go beyond ourselves and find the God within us. Therefore, when we start spiritual practice, we have to give up the habit of focusing on the five senses, mind and intellect, we have to erase those sanskars.

"पंचज्ञानेंद्रिय, मन, तथा बुद्धि पर हमारी निर्भरता तथा संबंधित संस्कारों को क्षीण करने का एक महत्त्वपूर्ण साधन है-प्रार्थना"।

Prayer includes respect, love, application and trust. Through prayer, the devotee accepts his inability and accepts God as the doer. Considering God as the doer in prayer means that our inner self accepts that God is helping us and also getting the work accomplished. Prayer is an important means of spiritual practice to move forward on the spiritual path of devotion (Bhaktiyoga).

The act of prayer shows that the power of the person to whom he is praying is higher than his own. Therefore, by praying a person expresses his weakness and seeks help from a higher power. This is like hurting one's ego since the meaning of prayer is that the person seeks help from someone higher in mind and wisdom than himself. In this way, by praying again and again, we are able to come out of our limited mind and intellect and contact the higher universal mind and universal intelligence. Doing this over time helps in getting our mind and intellect in tune. Thus, repeated and sincere prayer for spiritual progress helps in tuning the mind, intellect and ego.

2.1 Benefits of prayer

When we start our spiritual journey, we call it Sadhana and when we engage in prayer, it affects our Sadhana at three levels - action, thought and emotion:

- **Karma:** The work we do for spiritual benefit by praying is done emotionally. So make mistakes, mistakes are few. Therefore, various efforts of spiritual practice through prayer (like chanting, satsang, satseva etc.) are in accordance with the expectations of God or Guru (the guiding principle of God).
- **Thoughts:** As long as the mind remains active, the chain of thoughts continues. They hinder the merging of the mind. Useless thoughts also waste energy. Prayer is a very useful means to prevent this. Prayer reduces anxiety and increases contemplation.
- **Emotion:** Emotional prayer starts the thinking process in the seeker and helps him to become introverted.

Now we will try to understand which activities benefit from prayer-

- **Increase in the effect of chanting the name:** The seeker chants the name to attain God. Chanting the name is truly effective only when the desire and feeling of attaining God is intense. A saint would become so engrossed in chanting that he would not be aware of the outside world. It is rare to find someone who chants the name with such intensity. However, by repeatedly praying for excellent chanting, our feelings are awakened and our chanting reaches the feet of God.

- **Divine help in Sadhana:** When a seeker sincerely prays to God for some desired effort, thought and attitude to complement his Sadhana, then even the seemingly impossible task is easily accomplished by the grace of the Guru.

- **Getting forgiveness for mistakes:** If we pray to God or Guru with surrender after committing a mistake, then they forgive us. However, prayer and surrender should be commensurate with the severity of the mistake.

- **Ego diminishes:** While praying we plead before God. At that time, giving up our pride, we humbly accept our will, human weakness and dependence on God. As a result, our ego decreases quickly.
- **Protection from negative energies:** Prayer is a very effective means for protection from negative energies (ghosts, devils, vampire). This creates a protective shield all around the person praying.
- **Increase in faith:** When prayers are answered, faith in Guru and God also increases. The only currency in the journey of spiritual practice is faith.

(Source:Science of Spirituality)

2.2 Importance of Faith

Generally, unwavering faith in superiority is called faith. When faith turns from principle to practice, it is called loyalty. When loyalty enters the field of devotion to achieve the ultimate goal of a person's life, then it takes the form of devotion. In fact, faith is a quality which gives superiority to a person on the basis of his virtues, good thoughts and excellent characteristics. Only such virtuous and noble thoughts prove to be helpful as a ladder to take a person to the pinnacle of progress and illuminate his life path. The root of action, knowledge and worship or devotion is faith. Similarly, it is written in the book named Bhakti Rasamrit Sindhu that devotion not only enhances satsang, mutual harmony, affection, respect and cooperation, but also controls disunity in the society and increases the feeling of unity. The entire creation is an expression of God. Lord Shri Krishna has clearly declared at one place in 'Geeta' that only a person with faith can attain me. Any person in the materialistic world cannot attain God without faith. It is faith that creates speed, direction and harmony in the society and develops humanity.

Faith deeply affects every area of human life. It is said in Geeta that faith produces virtuous qualities in the spiritual field and royal qualities in the field of action. Saint Tulsidas has also said at one place in 'Manas' that 'There is no religion without faith'. In the field of devotion, faith has primacy. The energy acquired with faith and belief has amazing effects. Due to materialism and the influence of western civilization, we are forgetting our glorious past. In fact, faith is an excellent ornament of a person's life. That is why it is said that only devout people are able to attain knowledge. It should be remembered here that faith does not mean superstition. When superstition goes away, faith emerges.

Figure-2.2: Unique energy acquired with faith and belief

'Faith is the act of keeping the mind focused on good thoughts. This faith gives strength to man, inspires him in every way and makes life meaningful. The great poet Tulsidas in 'Manas' has said *'Bhavani Shankarau Vande, Shraddha-Vishwas Rupinau'* and has compared faith to Shiva and faith to Parvati, who always live together. Without their help, we cannot see the God present within us. There is a sense of determination in faith. When there is faith, the mind does not wander. Decides to follow a prescribed path. To reach the steps of success in worldly purposes, coordination of knowledge and action is sufficient, but spirituality is one step higher than this. For that there should also be a special reliance on faith. In this context, Geeta says that man is dependent on faith. Whatever faith one has, he becomes like the one who has considered himself evil, immoral, foolish etc., his same qualities and characteristics will continue to emerge and become visible. Similarly, the one who believes in himself as a saint, a gentleman and a great person, his same qualities are visible emerging and being implemented. In the absence of faith, Ganga is a river, Himalaya is a set of ice and stones and idol is a mere toy and Guru is a mere human being of ordinary level. Then God also appears to be just an invisible law of the natural system. Faith is actually life and form is its beauty (Figure-2.2).

If there is no faith then there is no difference between different animals, eg - cow and buffalo. Cow is like a revered mother for us whereas milk is obtained from both cow and buffalo. Shraddha mantras also appear to be a set of letters. A saint lived on the banks of Ganga. In case there was no boat, he would recite the Ram Mantra in the ears of those crossing and say, 'Cross the Ganga while chanting this.' There lived a fakir some distance away, he also performed similar miracles. If those coming down had been asked to take the name of God, they too would have crossed. A clever person figured out how to penetrate both and by combining both, he could overcome the situation more easily. He started trying to cross saying 'Ram-Khuda' and drowned in the middle of the Ganges. Power is not in words, but in the feelings associated with them, in the capsule of faith in power.

2.2.1 Faith is the foundation of human life: As one has faith, so does his personality become. In the words of the lyricist, 'Shraddhamayoyaam Purushah', this man is devout by nature. It is a different matter what the basis of his faith should be. Just as there is no day without the sun, nothing can be seen without eyes, nothing can be heard without ears, similarly life cannot progress without faith. Just as love is necessary for a lamp to remain lit, similarly devotion is required for life. That man is not a human being who does not have faith.

2.2.2 Only faith enables one to realize the truth: 'Shraddhaya Satyamapyate' (Yaju. 19.30) Truth is attained through faith. 'Shraddha Praanh' (Atharva 9.5.21) Faith is the life of man. A person without faith should be considered lifeless and lifeless. Because without any kind of faith, he will remain inactive and a life without effort is like death.

Faith is the basis of liberation, attainment of knowledge and practice of life. The lyricist has said-

> **'श्रद्धावन् लभते ज्ञान तत्परः संयतेन्द्रियः।**
> **ज्ञानं लब्ध्वा पराँशान्तिमचिरेणाधि गच्छति ॥'**

A devout person easily acquires knowledge by controlling his senses. On attaining knowledge one attains liberation and then one experiences ultimate peace and happiness.

Our faith originates from some important personality. When we see a special quality or power in a person compared to the common people, a joyful attraction towards him arises in us. This attraction, along with accepting his importance, also creates in us a feeling of worship towards him. The name of this process is faith.

2.2.3 A person's qualities and actions are the basis of faith: Therefore, the actions that generate faith are called religion and the condition of human society is determined by this religion. In short, a religious person is the center of our faith. This religion (karma) is the main motive between the devotee and the revered.

A person's talent, power and resourcefulness can also be the basis of faith, but this is not a universal rule. Regarding these, there is no certainty that they will be beneficial for the society.

Even a talented person can exploit the society and cause harm to it. Despite being powerful, a man can be a hooligan, a wicked person, a misdemeanor. Even a person with resources can do evil and harm to the society. Therefore, actions which hinder social welfare cannot be the basis for full respect for a human being. However, there are some people in the society who praise terrorists. A talented person, despite being an addict and a misdemeanor, can be the center of respect for some people. A resourceful person can become the object of respect for many people even by doing anti-social activities. But since all these are harmful for the society, they cannot be the right basis for our faith. On the contrary, being devoted towards such people and encouraging them means becoming a partaker of the sinful tendencies committed by them, that is, becoming a partaker of sin.

Therefore, only good deeds, morality, modesty and gentleness can be the appropriate basis for our faith because it is related to the welfare of human beings. The condition of the society gets strengthened by these. In their absence, even talent and resourcefulness can be harmful.

Gentleness, modesty and the good deeds inspired by it, which can also be called religion in other words, are respected in all the communities of the world and they help in the rules, order and condition of the society. Therefore these can be the true basis of our faith.

Where faith forms the basis of a person's personal life, works as an inspiration, clarifies the mysteries of life and provides liberation, it is also an important social duty. If we do not have respect for a virtuous, well-mannered and religious person, we do not perform our duties. If we do not express feelings of thanks and gratitude when we see someone doing good work, taking a courageous step, or practicing religion, then we are like a stone to the society. We are of no use to him. Therefore faith is a social responsibility. This gives strength to religion and life to nobility. Just as a tree needs to be watered to keep it green, similarly to keep the society full of good deeds and religious, it needs to be watered with devotion.

2.2.4 Reverence is actually a social feeling: it is a 'joyful gratitude' that we reveal to the society as a representative. There is no question of giving or taking in faith. This is a social responsibility. It is the religion of the common people. Any person can be worthy of respect if he is useful for social life.

Through faith, we not only do good for ourselves but also do great good to the society. A virtuous, religious person by nature wants to see the presence of happiness and joy around him and we express our joy and happiness by expressing our devotion. This increases the enthusiasm of the devotee. He is aware of his capabilities. This encourages modesty, morality and religion in the society, which are necessary for the security of the society.

2.2.5 Faith is not a thing to be said or preached: By having faith in someone in our mind, we can help in giving prestige to his importance in the society even when we live far away. The basis of faith is virtues and deeds. Man is secondary. We can strengthen those virtues and dharma anywhere with devotion by practicing them ourselves and spreading them among others. In this context there is no need to say 'I have respect for you.'

Who has lost everything, who is disappointed with life and faith gives solace, support and life. Every capable person is also incomplete in himself, he needs some support and faith is the pure support of man. There is such 'trust in others' that even one's own work becomes easier. The life of the devotee becomes easier. The heat of his life cools down. Difficulties become ineffective with the support of faith. Those people whose life is devoid of faith, easy paths are closed in their life, they have to resort to the painful path of difficulties or they are able to cover only a short distance in a long time. But nothing remains difficult or impossible for those who acquire faith.

2.2.6 The foundation of faith is to accept the importance of others: In any field, we give importance to a person by being influenced by his characteristics, in such a situation we have to forget our self. But people who are full of selfishness and narrow-mindedness, who like to boast about themselves, who do not value anyone except themselves, such selfish and arrogant people do not develop a feeling of reverence. Due to their narrow-mindedness, these people are not able to realistically evaluate the work and life of others.

2.2.7 Faith depends on justice and intellect: The greater the virtues and deeds of the revered person, the greater the faith in other people. The true evaluation of virtue, good deeds, modesty and adherence to religion is faith. Faith is not a business in which the devotee expects to get something from the devotee. This is a sacred medium between two persons. If we express our respect towards someone with the intention of achieving some desire, then it is not respect but flattery. In the name of faith, one has to deceive oneself and the devotee. There is no doubt that nowadays such false devotees and devotees are more prevalent.

The scripture writers have unanimously said that only deeds done with devotion, donations given etc. are successful. Any work done without faith becomes futile.

The lyricist has said-

'अश्रद्धया हुतं दत्तं तपस्तप्तं कृतं च यत्।
असदित्युच्यते पार्थ न च तत्प्रेत्य नो इह॥'

'Yagya performed without faith, penance done by charity, even any work does not yield results, it goes in vain. Oh Arjun, if you don't get any success in this world, then what will you get in the next world?'

There is description in Rigveda-

श्रद्धायाग्नि समिध्यसे, श्रद्धा हूयते हविः।
श्रद्धा भगस्य मूर्धिनि वचसा वेदयामसि॥

2.2.8 The fire of the soul gets lit by faith: sacrifice is made in it only with faith. Faith is at the top of all welfare works, without faith nothing is achieved.

Upanishadkar has also said the same-Shraddhayadayam (should be given with devotion)

श्रद्धयादयम् (श्रद्धापूर्वक देना चाहिए)

Whatever is given with reverence to a devotee is called charity. Well, there are two motivations for charity – one is faith and the other is kindness. The motivation to donate to powerless, poor and helpless people arises from compassion, but the motivation to give to capable people arises from the inspiration of faith. The only true thing is to readily fill the void of men engaged in imparting knowledge, engaged in social service and philanthropy, engaged in increasing the knowledge of the human community. It goes right into the heart of the society and nourishes all the parts of the society. But what is given to selfish, hypocritical and unjust people does not seem to be a part of the society in the same way as water is not stored in a pot with holes.

Selfish people are seen using faith for their own benefit or to satisfy their base desires. Some wear the clothes of saints and some raise slogans of public service, while some deceive the society by pretending to be great sacrificers. Such people say lofty things as if they are a great scholar or a wise meditator. By influencing innocent people through various kinds of fabrications, publicity and propaganda, they gain their trust and then exploit that society for their own benefit.

Many people use faith as a means of their enjoyment. For such people, reverence is the same as liquor, cannabis, ganja, Chandu etc. are for drug addicts. Such people cannot bear the separation of their name from their works even for a moment. These people take up such work in which there is a lot of pomp and show about the name and work but there is nothing in the original. But reverence is not for such misuse and extravagance. We should take utmost care in this regard. No person with corrupt mentality should be able to exploit our feelings of faith and misuse it. Because all our powers can also be misused through faith. Faith is a nectar that strengthens the society, but it is also the duty of the society that wicked and selfish people should not misuse it.

With this caution let us worship with faith.

श्रद्धाँ प्रार्प्यहवाभहे श्रद्धाँ मध्यदिन परि।
श्रद्धाँ सूर्यस्य निम्रुचि श्रेद्धे श्रद्धापयह नः॥ (ऋ. 0। 051। 5)

Invoke Shraddha Devi. Let us be full of faith in the morning. Be reverent in the afternoon. Be full of faith in the evening and remain full of faith even at night. Maintain faith in every task of life, in every moment.

2.3 Smile

In the ancient Vedic scriptures and rules, every day begins with the recitation of auspicious mantras. If any person follows the mantra rules properly with a happy heart, his life is filled with happiness and good fortune. Due to happy mind, qualitative energy is transmitted in the body and you do not feel tired while working. You can do any difficult task with ease. Therefore, every person should go about his daily routine smiling and happy.

It is also said that in the hectic daily routine, many things related to work and family make you mentally tired and cause stress. If you are a victim of mental stress and want to get rid of it, then do your work with a smile and you will definitely get success.

Have you ever wondered why you were shaking before your exams or why your palms were sweaty before a job interview? These feelings of worry or anxiety are the body's natural way of preparing itself for an important event. You may also have noticed how once the event begins, you start to calm down, your breathing becomes easier and your heart stops racing. Such worries actually help us perform better because they make us more alert.

But some people may feel anxious or nervous for no apparent reason. If you find it difficult to control your worries and the persistent feeling of worry interferes with your ability to perform everyday tasks, this condition is called anxiety. Or anxiety can be called a disease. In such a situation, do your work with a smile, you will definitely get success.

2.3.1 Symptoms of Anxiety

Everyone has anxiety or panic, so it's hard to know when it might be diagnosed as a disorder. If your anxiety impairs your functioning over a period of time, you should seek the advice of a mental health professional. There are many types of anxiety disorders but their common symptoms are as follows-

- Increase in heart rate, shortness of breath.
- Increased tension in the nerves.

- Feeling of strain in the chest.
- Increase in baseless and irrational worries and restlessness or anxiety.
- Increasing inclination towards unnecessary things which leads to stubbornness in behaviour.

If you notice these signs in a friend or family member, you should talk to them about their possible condition and recommend that they see a mental health professional.

2.3.2 Reasons for concern

Family history: People with a family history of mental health problems are more likely to develop anxiety disorders. For example, a disorder called OCD can be passed from one generation to the next.

- **Stressful events:** Stress at work, death of a loved one, breakdown in relationships, etc. can also trigger symptoms of anxiety.
- **Health related issues**: Thyroid problems, asthma, diabetes or heart disease can cause anxiety. People suffering from depression can also fall prey to anxiety disorders. For example, a person who has been suffering from depression for a long time, his performance starts declining. This increases work related stress and then gives rise to anxiety.
- **Drug use:** People who become addicted to drugs, alcohol or any other substance on a large scale also suffer from anxiety. When the effects of intoxication start wearing off, anxiety starts increasing.
- **Personality-related causes:** Sometimes, people with certain personalities, such as perfectionists or people who want to be in control, may also develop nervousness and anxiety issues.

2.3.3 Types of concern

Anxiety or nervousness affects people in different ways, causing many types of disorders. The most common and common disorders among these are as follows:

- **Generalized anxiety disorder:** Generalized anxiety disorder (GAD) – People with GAD experience excessive anxiety and worry during various situations and events. They are unable to control their anxieties. They start feeling restless and always feel like they are stuck or on the edge. Such people are not worried or anxious about any particular thing and there is no specific reason for the emergence of these emotions.
- **Obsessive Compulsive Disorder:** Obsessive Compulsive Disorder (OCD) – People suffering from OCD have persistent thoughts or fears that increase their anxiety. They keep repeating the same actions to get rid of this anxious situation or to get relief from it. For example, a person who is fearful of germs and infection will constantly wash his hands or household utensils.
- **Fear of society:** Social phobia or social anxiety disorder, Social Anxiety Disorder (SAD) – People suffering from this type of disorder are afraid of social or public performance situations. They feel afraid of going into the society because they feel that they will be tested there i.e. they will be exposed in front of other people. They have a deep fear that whatever they say or do will insult them and cause them embarrassment. Such people are unable to handle everyday situations like giving a small talk, giving a short speech or eating in a public place.
- **Specific fear or phobia:** Phobias are irrational and unfounded fears, and people who have them try to avoid things or situations that cause unnecessary fear in order to avoid feeling anxious or nervous. They are afraid of everything from traveling by plane, going into crowded places to seeing spiders and tall buildings.

- **Post-traumatic stress disorder (PTSD):** Experiencing or witnessing extreme torture or trauma, or physical assault, can lead to PTSD. The person suffering from this disorder does not sleep, he is also not able to rest properly because he keeps remembering old things again and again (flashback of the incident) (Figure-2.3).

Figure-2.3: Passing through or witnessing an event

Panic disorder: People with panic disorder have sudden fear attacks that are uncontrolled and include many physical symptoms such as dizziness, shortness of breath, and excessive sweating. On such occasions, they may also complain of psychological symptoms such as a feeling of impending doom or distress and suicidal feelings such as I am about to die or I am going crazy. These seizures do not occur for any apparent reason and the person is constantly worried about such seizures occurring again.

2.3.4 Importance of smile

We all know that smiling does not cost money but it is a sign of happiness and prosperity. Now, through Vipassana, you not only get all the benefits on group of deceases but also get freedom from its side effects while start chanting any word or mantra or the name of any god or saint for whom you have faith in your mind. No part of the body will remain unconscious or semi-conscious (Figure: 2.4).

Figure 2.4: Smiling – a sign of happiness and prosperity

You may not know these benefits of smiling

- If you are a teacher and when you enter the class smiling, you will see smiles on the faces of all the children.
- If you are a doctor and treat the patient with a smile, the patient's confidence will double.
- If you are a housewife then do every household work with a smile, then it will create an atmosphere of happiness in the entire family.
- If you are the head of the house, then if you enter the house in the evening smiling, it will create an atmosphere of happiness in the entire family.
- If you are a businessman and you enter the company happy, then you will see that the pressure in the minds of all the employees will reduce and the atmosphere will become pleasant.
- If you are a shopkeeper and respect your customer by smiling, then the customer will be happy and buy goods from your shop.
- Sometimes smile at a stranger while walking on the road, see that a smile will appear on his face too.

2.3.5 Smile-Because

- Smiling does not cost money, it is a sign of happiness and prosperity.
- Your smile will bring smile on many faces.
- You will not get this life again.

- Blessings given in anger also seem bad and bad words said with a smile also seem good.
- Every person in the world likes blooming flowers and smiling faces.
- Your laughter can become the reason for someone's happiness.
- Relationships in a family can last only as long as we keep smiling at each other.

2.3.6 One Biggest Thing

Smile, because this is the hallmark of being human. An animal can never smile. Therefore, smile yourself and bring smile on the faces of others too, this is life and happiness is life.

5.

Yoga Mudras and its Importance

Yoga Mudra is an ancient technique, which we practice during Praanyam and meditation. Mudra is a Sanskrit word meaning attitude. In ancient times, sages used to perform Yoga Mudras to balance the five elements present inside the body: air, water, fire, earth and sky. Our fingers are characterized by these elements and each of these five elements has a specific and important function within the body. This is the reason why even today people practice yoga postures. This is a branch of Yoga which is less popular, independent and subtle/deep branch, its name is – Yoga Tattva Mudra ViGyaan. As we practice yoga, we begin to feel its subtle effects on the body, mind and consciousness.

Thus Yoga Mudras are a set of physical activities that change the mind, attitude and perception of a person. Yoga Mudras work to flow energy to specific parts of the brain. Generally, many elements present in our body are not in balanced state due to which various types of diseases occur in the body and the person starts suffering from mild to serious diseases and problems. In such a situation, Yoga Mudra works to balance the five elements of the body and also helps in keeping the entire body healthy.

Highly specific and based on the principles of Ayurveda, Yoga Mudras are considered healing tools, the Sanskrit word mudra meaning body gesture or attitude. The entire body or only the hands are used for the pose. Practicing the postures along with yogic breathing stimulates different parts of the body and alerts the flow of Praan in the body. Practicing the postures along with yogic breathing stimulates different parts of the body and alerts the flow of Praan in the body.

3.1 Types of Yoga Mudras

We know that there are five elements present in the body and due to imbalance of these elements a person becomes vulnerable to diseases. The properties of these five elements are inherent in the fingers of our hands. Among the five fingers of the hand, air is situated on the index finger, water on the little finger, fire on the thumb, earth on the ring finger and sky (space) on the middle Finger (Figure-3.1).

Based on these, yoga mudras are divided into five groups and they usually depend on the body parts practiced.

Hatha Yoga Pradipika and Gheranda Samhita are the main texts on Mudras. There are 10 descriptions of postures in Hathayoga Pradipika and 25 postures in Gherand Samhita. Some yoga mudras are easy for us. We can influence our attitude and thinking just by touching the hands with fingers. And that's where you can heal your body with your inner strength.

In general, mudras can be divided into five groups.

- Hand Mudra
- Head Mudra
- Sitting Mudra
- Bandha (lock posture)
- Base Mudra

Although as mentioned above there are hundreds of types of yoga mudras, but different yoga mudras are practiced to cure different diseases present in the body.

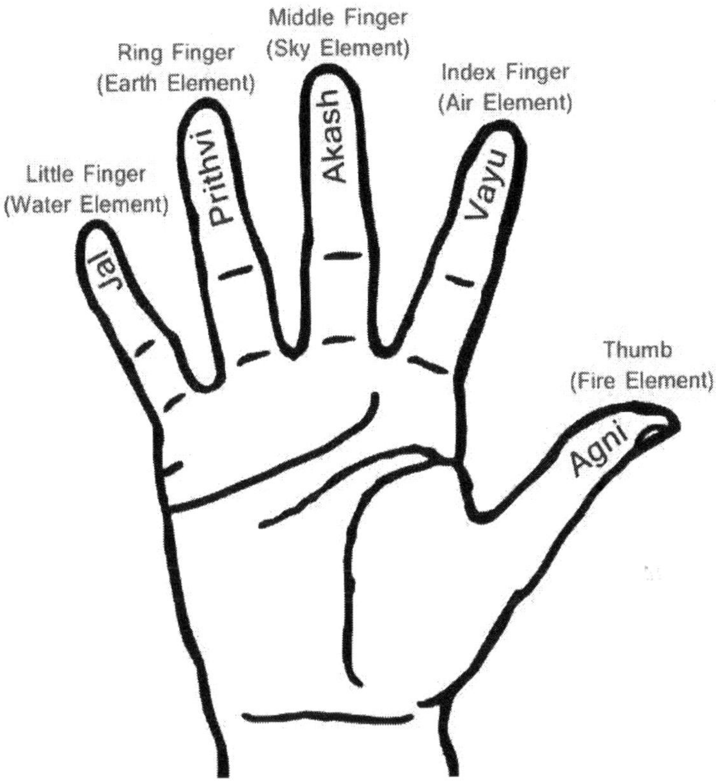

Figure-3.1: Yoga Mudra – Properties of the five elements in the fingers of the hands

3.2 Some Yoga Mudras and its Benefits

Usually yoga mudras depend on different parts of the body but since the five elements found in the body are mentioned only with the fingers, Hasta Yoga postures are more popular. Let us know some easy and important yoga mudras and their benefits like: Pran, Gyaan, Suryaa, Vayu Mudras (Fig.3.2).

3.2.1 Praan Mudra

Praan Mudra is done to balance the life element of a person's body. This yoga posture improves the immune system and protects the body from diseases. It is also considered an important posture as it fills the body with energy.

Method of Doing Praan Mudra

- Sit comfortably and slightly bend your ring finger and little finger and touch them with the tip of the thumb.
- Keep the other two fingers of the hand straight upwards.
- Now place your palm above the knee.
- Relax your hands and shoulders and close your eyes and sit in this posture for some time.

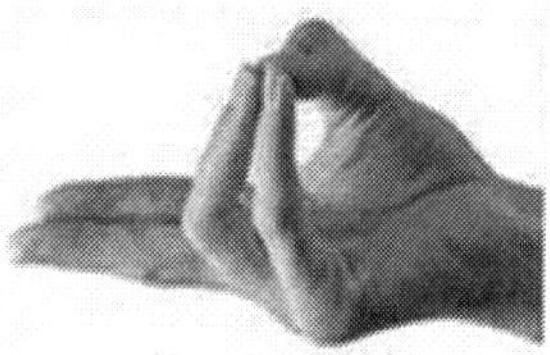

Praan Mudra

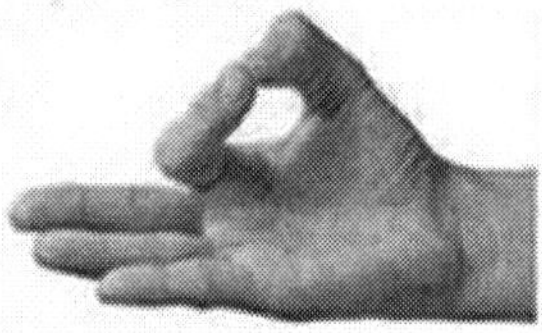

Gyaan Mudra

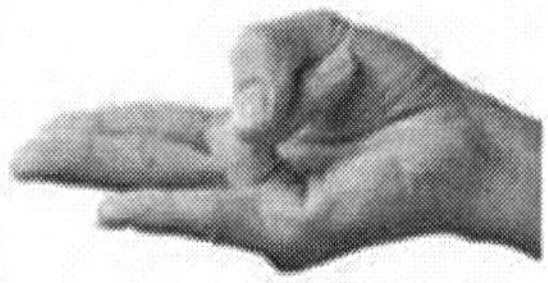

Suryaa Mudra

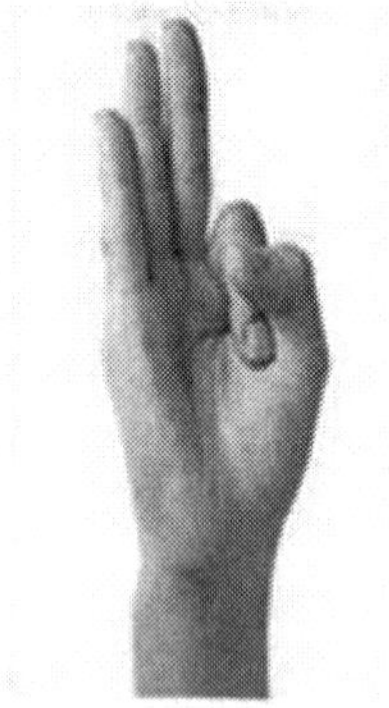

Vaayu Mudra

Figure-3.2: Important Yoga Mudras (Praan, Gyaan, Suryaa and Vayu Mudras) and benefits

Benefits of Praan Mudra

- Practicing Praan Mudra strengthens the immune system.
- Practicing this mudra daily improves eyesight and sharpens vision.

- This mudra is very beneficial for removing eye diseases and eye fatigue.
- This mudra also has many benefits in keeping the body active.
- This mudra is very beneficial in removing vitamin deficiency in the body, protecting from diseases and making the internal organs functional.

3.2.2 Gyaan Mudra

This is the most basic yoga mudra that helps in improving concentration and wisdom.

How to Exchange Knowledge

- Sit comfortably on the floor in Padmasana posture.
- After this, bend the index finger and place it on the thumb.
- Keep the other three fingers straight and these three fingers should not touch each other.
- Now place the hand above the knee and keep the palm slightly bent below the knee.
- Do not put any tension on your hands and sit in this posture for some time with your eyes closed.

Benefits of Gyaan Mudra

- Gyaan Mudra is very beneficial in removing the problem of insomnia.
- This posture increases concentration and also strengthens memory power.
- By practicing Gyaan Mudra daily, psychological problems like anger, depression, stress and anxiety go away.
- This posture increases energy in the body and is very beneficial in providing relief from back pain.

3.2.3 Suryaa Mudra

This posture helps in balancing the Suryaa element in the person's body. To take advantage of the sun's energy, this mudra should be done early in the morning.

How to do Suryaa Mudra

- Sit comfortably on the ground.
- Bend your ring finger from the middle and place the tip of the thumb on it and apply light pressure with the thumb on the ring finger.
- Keep the remaining fingers of the palm straight and do not bend them.
- Practice this posture daily for half an hour early in the morning.

Benefits of Suryaa Mudra

- By practicing Suryaa Mudra, weight remains under control and there is no problem of obesity.
- This mudra increases the fire element in the body and helps in maintaining balanced body temperature.
- Suryaa Mudra works effectively in preventing digestive problems, loss of appetite, trembling, extreme cold in hands and feet.
- This mudra is also beneficial in reducing cholesterol and improving digestion.

3.2.4 Vayu Mudra

As the name suggests, Vayu Mudra is done to maintain the balance of air in the body.

How to do Vayu Mudra

- Bend your index finger.
- After this, bend the index finger at the base of your thumb and press the bone and keep it near the base.
- Keep the other three fingers of the hand straight and do not put any pressure on the fingers.
- After this, place the palm on the knee and close the eyes and sit for some time.

Benefits of Vayu Mudra

- This posture works to expel excess air from the body and helps in relieving chest pain caused by gas.
- Regular practice of Vayu Mudra removes nervousness and restlessness and keeps the mind calm.
- This mudra is effective in removing Vata Dosha and provides relief from arthritis, gas problem, sciatica, knee and muscle pain.
- Apart from this, this mudra is also beneficial in removing the problem of sneezing and yawning.

3.2.5 Shoonya (Zero) Mudra

This mudra is also called Swarga Mudra and the practice of this posture gives a strange kind of peace to the mind.

Shoonya Mudra Method

- Sit comfortably on the floor.
- After this, bend your middle finger near the middle bone and place the tip of your thumb on top of the nail of this finger.
- Keep the remaining three fingers of the hand i.e. index finger, ring finger and little finger straight and apart from each other.
- Now keep the hand hanging lightly on the ground above the knee.
- Keep your hands and shoulders in a relaxed posture and sit quietly with your eyes closed for some time.

Benefits of Shoonya Mudra

By practicing Shoonya (Zero) Mudra, the problem of hearing loss or deafness is cured to a great extent. Apart from this, this Mudra is also beneficial in relieving ear pain. This mudra is beneficial in heart disease, throat problems, watery eyes and keeping bones strong.

3.2.6 Varun Mudra

This posture helps in maintaining the balance of water element in the body. Works to brighten the face as the fluids present in the body flow properly and it moisturizes the face well.

How to do Varuna Mudra

- Sit comfortably on the floor and bend your little finger and thumb slightly and touch each other's knuckles.
- Keep the remaining fingers of the hand straight.
- After this, bend the palm slightly like the ground and place it on the thigh.
- Close your eyes and sit in this posture for some time.
- While doing this mudra, take special care not to press the knuckles with the nails, otherwise instead of balancing the water element in the body, you may face the problem of dehydration.

Benefits of Varun Mudra

- This mudra is very beneficial in keeping the mind calm and curing skin related diseases.
- Practicing Varun Mudra daily helps in proper circulation of fluids in the body due to which the person does not get infection and also gets rid of acne.
- This Varun Mudra gives relief from muscle pain and brings natural glow to the face.

3.2.7 Apan Mudra - Method, Benefits and Precautions

What is Apan Mudra?

The place of Apan is the center of health and strength. If we talk about yoga here, then in yoga it is called Muladhar Chakra. This posture makes the heart powerful. That is why it is also called Hridaya Mudra. The function of Apan is to expel stool, urine, semen, womb and semen. It helps in dynamic situations like sleeping, sitting, getting up, walking etc. Just as earning is essential for life, similarly immersion is also essential for life.

Method of Doing Apan Mudra

1) First of all, spread a mat on the ground and sit on it in Padmasana or Siddhasana, making sure that your spine is straight.
2) Place both your hands on your knees and the palms should be towards the sky.
3) Now bend the index finger of your hand and place it on the tip of the thumb and touch the first knuckle of the middle and ring fingers with the first knuckle of the thumb and press lightly and keep the little finger straight.
4) You should practice by concentrating on your breathing. Breathing has to be kept normal during exercise.
5) This state should remain for at least 48 minutes.

Method of Doing Apan Mudra

1) First of all, spread a mat on the ground and sit on it in Padmasana or Siddhasana, making sure that your spine is straight.
2) Place both your hands on your knees and the palms should be towards the sky.
3) Now bend the index finger of your hand and place it on the tip of the thumb and touch the first knuckle of the middle and ring fingers with the first knuckle of the thumb and press lightly and keep the little finger straight.
4) You should practice by concentrating on your breathing. Breathing has to be kept normal during exercise.
5) This state should remain for at least 48 minutes.

Time and Duration of Apan Mudra

If you practice this every day, you will get good results. Practicing this mudra in the morning and evening is more fruitful. Mudra can be practiced in the morning, afternoon and evening for 16 minutes each.

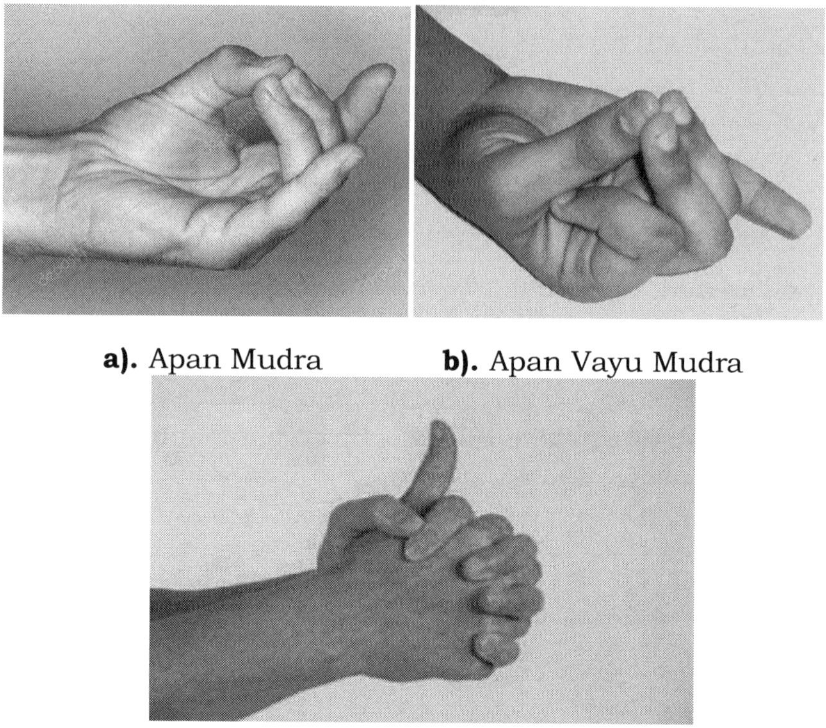

a). Apan Mudra **b).** Apan Vayu Mudra

c). Linga Mudra

Figure-3.2: Important yoga postures a). Apan Mudra, b). Apan Vayu Mudra and c). Linga Mudra and its benefits

Health Benefits of Apan Mudra

Mudra provides relief from all heart diseases.

1) By practicing it regularly, respiratory diseases are cured.
2) Provides relief from diseases like indigestion, gas, acidity, constipation etc.
3) Relation to stomach cures all diseases.
4) By doing this, dental diseases are cured.
5) By practicing it regularly, the tubes of the body get purified.
6) The impurities and impurities are dissolved and purity is achieved.

7) It removes urinary disorders.
8) Cures diabetes.
9) All the toxic elements come out of the body.
10) Pregnant women benefit from it.
11) Reduces body weight.
12) This posture removes body heat by inducing sweating.

Caution during Apan Mudra

This Apan Mudra should be done on an empty stomach. While doing this mudra, your attention should not get distracted. Apan Mudra is a powerful mudra in which three elements are combined together with the fire element, hence it should not be done more than a certain time. By doing this there is a possibility of more urine coming out. It doesn't cause any harm so don't be afraid of it.

3.2.8 Apanvayu Mudra - Method, Benefits and Precautions

What is Apanvayu mudra

Another name for Apanvayu Mudra is Mrita-Sanjeevani Mudra. It is directly related to the heart. Apan Vayu Mudra is made up of two mudras, one is Vayu Mudra which helps us in reducing the increased gas in the stomach. And the second one is Apan Mudra which keeps our heart healthy. And this mudra also increases the digestive power. Therefore it is also known as Hridaya Mudra. Doing this mudra during a sudden heart attack provides immediate relief to the patient.

In this mudra, two mudras are applied together – Vayu Mudra and Apan Mudra. That is why its compound name is – Apan Vayu Mudra. Due to it being very beneficial in heart attack, it has also been given the name of Mrit Sanjeevani Mudra. If we call it Apan Vayu Mudra then it becomes easy to remember the method of this Mudra – Vayu Mudra Apan Mudra.

Vayu Mudra is a painkiller – natural PAIN KILLER, if there is pain anywhere in the body, gas problem, Vayu Mudra cures it.

Apan Mudra strengthens the digestive power and heart. ANGINA PECTORIS This is a powerful mudra for heart pain.

Method of doing Apan Vayu Mudra

1. First of all, spread a mat on the ground and sit on it in Padmasana or Siddhasana, making sure that your spine is straight.
2. Place both your hands on your knees and the palms should be towards the sky.
3. Now bend the index finger of your hand and place it at the root of the thumb and touch the first knuckle of the middle and ring fingers with the first knuckle of the thumb and press lightly and leave the little finger straight.
4. You should practice by concentrating on your breathing. Breathing has to be kept normal during exercise.
5. This state should remain for at least 48 minutes.

Time and duration of doing Apan Vayu Mudra

If you practice this every day, you will get good results. Practicing this mudra in the morning and evening is more fruitful. Mudra can be practiced in the morning, afternoon and evening for 16 minutes each.

Benefits of Apan Vayu Mudra

1. Apan Vayu Mudra has a special effect on the heart. This mudra is immediately beneficial in preventing heart attack and also in case of heart attack. This mudra works like a sorbitate pill – the benefits of this mudra start within two to three seconds. The patient gets miraculous relief. Due to increased air, the blood vessels of the heart start becoming dry – they start shrinking. Blood circulation in the heart reduces. Vayu Mudra removes the contraction of the heart vessels. And blood circulation in the heart increases.

2. Heart colic goes away.
3. All heart diseases are cured.
4. Both high blood pressure and low blood pressure are cured.
5. Whether the heartbeat increases or slows down – in both the situations it normalizes the heartbeat.
6. Beneficial in anxiety and all diseases of the nervous system.
7. Makes lungs healthy – Beneficial in asthma.
8. Immediate relief in rheumatic diseases – flatulence, gas, stomach ache, anal disease, acidity, heartburn due to gas are all cured.
9. Headache, half headache, headache are actually caused by stomach upset. This posture has miraculous benefits in headache. Diseases caused by insomnia or excessive exertion are also cured.
10. Relief from knee pain – By doing Apan Vayu Mudra for 5 to 7 minutes before climbing the stairs, you will neither feel breathless nor have pain in your knees while climbing the stairs.
11. Hiccups stop. Also beneficial in toothache.
12. Unexplained blinking of eyes also stops. In our culture, twitching of the right eye of women and the left eye of men is considered inauspicious. Apanvayu Mudra is beneficial in this.
13. Removes all three defects - Vata-Pitta-Kapha. Circulatory system, digestive system heals everything.
14. Removes all negative pressure from body and mind. According to Acharya Keshavdev ji, continuous practice of this mudra prevents all types of heart diseases, but along with the mudra, it is also necessary to pay attention to your food, daily routine, exercise etc. This mudra is a panacea for heart disease. Even more beneficial than an effective injection.
15. While eating, if any particle of food enters the windpipe, it causes difficulty in breathing. Death can occur due to

respiratory arrest within a minute or two. In such emergency situations, this mudra is very effective, you will get immediate relief, this experience is of Dr. Ramesh Puri himself.

16. In case of heart attack, 70 percent people die before reaching the hospital – famous cardiologist Dr. K.K. Aggarwal says that death can be avoided by immediately applying Mritasanjeevani Mudra in case of heart attack.

Caution during Apan Vayu Mudra

This Apan Vayu Mudra should be done on an empty stomach. While doing this mudra, your attention should not get distracted. Apan Vayu Mudra is a powerful mudra in which three elements are combined together with the fire element, hence it should not be done for more than a certain time and this mudra should be done twice a day for 16-16 minutes only. Doing Vajrasana while sitting gives quick relief from heart disease.

3.2.9 Linga Mudra - Method, Benefits and Precautions

What is Ling Mudra

This posture is a symbol of masculinity, that is why it is called Linga Mudra. Linga Mudra is practiced to increase body heat. This is the most effective mudra to get rid of cough and phlegm. To do this mudra, you have to interlace the fingers of both your hands and keep the thumb (either left or right) straight. This mudra is practiced a lot in winter. By using Linga Mudra in your household life, you can reduce obesity by removing unnecessary calories from your body. If you feel too much cold in the body or there is cold obstruction, using Linga Mudra gives quick relief. Doing this for a long time causes sweating even in winter.

Method of Doing Linga Mudra

1. First of all, spread a mat on the ground and sit on it in Padmasana or Siddhasana, making sure that your spine is straight.
2. Now interlace the fingers of both your hands, keep one thumb straight and bring the other thumb straight from behind the thumb and make a circle.
3. Keep your eyes closed and make your breathing normal.
4. Keep your mind focused on your breathing speed and posture.
5. And this position should remain for at least 16 minutes.

Time and Duration of Doing Linga Mudra

If you practice this every day, you will get good results. Practicing this mudra in the morning and evening is more fruitful. Vayu Mudra can be practiced for 16-16 minutes in the morning and evening.

Benefits of Linga Mudra

1. By practicing it regularly, the seeker gets energized and enthusiastic.
2. This mudra protects the celibacy of the person.
3. Makes personality calm and attractive.
4. This mudra is very beneficial to avoid cold.
5. Doing this provides relief from fever caused by cold.
6. By using this mudra, irregularities related to menstrual discharge of women are cured.
7. Diseases like catarrh, cold, sinusitis, asthma and low blood pressure are eliminated.
8. Regular practice burns extra calories.
9. Weight is reduced from the body.
10. The deviated navel comes back to its place.
11. This posture strengthens the respiratory system.
12. This mudra relieves the problem of phlegm and cough.

13. It provides relief from the problem of heartburn.
14. Provides strength to the lungs.

Precautions in Linga Mudra

This Linga Mudra should be done on an empty stomach. Your attention should not get distracted while doing this mudra. Those who have bile problem should not do this mudra. This posture should not be done for a long time during the summer season.

3.2.10 Agni Mudra - Method, Benefits and Precautions

What is Agni Mudra

It is a posture that helps in the release of locked energy within the body and directs the flow and reflexes of the brain. When hands are intentionally held in a particular configuration, neuronal circuits are stimulated over a long period of time that reinforce the specific effects of the posture on the brain. Let us know its benefits and how to do this mudra:-

Method of doing Agni Mudra

- First of all, spread the carpet/mat on a clean and flat place. Now sit in Sukhasana, Padmasana or Vajrasana.
- Now extend the thumbs of both your hands and make a fist with your fingers.
- Then join the tips of the thumbs of both your hands together. And keep your palms downwards.
- Keeping your eyes closed, make your breathing normal and keep your mind focused on your breathing speed and posture.
- Now remain in this position for 15-45 minutes.

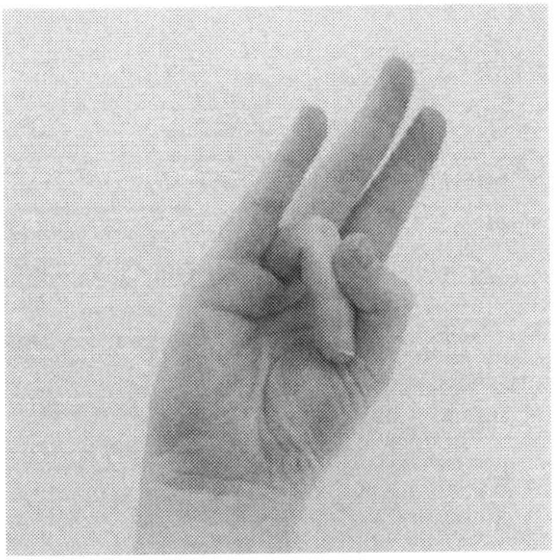

a). Fire Mudra

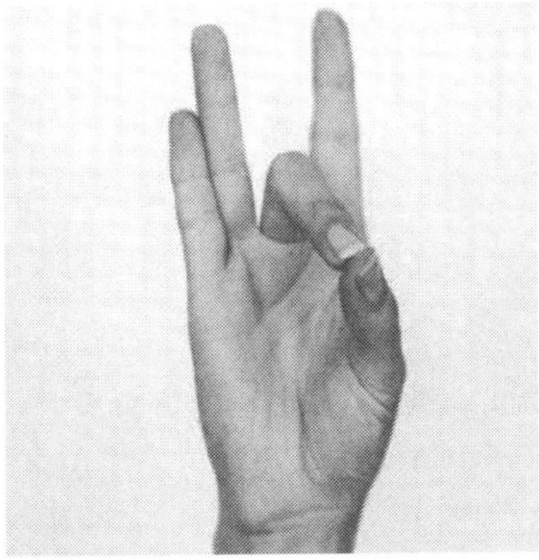

b). Earth Mudra

Figure-3.3: Important Yoga Mudras- a). Agni Mudra, b). Prithvi Mudra and Their Advantages

Time and duration of doing Agni Mudra

If you practice this every day, you will get good results. Practicing this mudra in the morning and evening is more fruitful. Agni Mudra can be practiced for 15 to 45 minutes.

Benefits of Agni Mudra

- This mudra is very beneficial in headache and migraine.
- Beneficial for all problems related to low blood pressure.
- Beneficial for hunger problem.
- Helps in reducing obesity.
- Doing this provides relief from problems like phlegm and cough.
- The complaint of pneumonia goes away.
- By doing this the amount of Agni in the body increases.

Precautions in Agni Mudra

This Agni Mudra should be done on an empty stomach. Your attention should not get distracted while doing this mudra.

3.2.11 Prithvi Mudra - Method, Benefits and Precautions

What is Prithvi Mudra?

Prithvi Mudra is called Gesture of the Earth in English. Its other name is Agni Shamak Mudra. Through this, man awakens the earth element in his physical core and helps in reducing the increasing fire element in the body. When this mudra is done then the earth elements increase and become even. By practicing this mudra new components are formed. There are two nadis in the human body, Suryaa Nadi and Chandra Nadi. When Prithvi Mudra is done, pressure is applied on the ring finger i.e. Suryaa finger, which helps in activating the Suryaa Nadi and Swara.

- The engagement finger symbolizes the earth element. Earth element gives us solidity and stability. This increases the earth element.
- The engagement finger is considered to be the center of all vitamins and life force.
- The engaged finger conducts strong electrical current all the time and so does the thumb.
- We apply Tilak on the engagement finger only. Perform puja and wear ring in marriage.

Method of doing Prithvi Mudra

- First of all, sit in Padmasana or Sukhasana position.
- Now place both your hands on your knees.
- Now bend your index finger or little finger and touch it with the tip of your thumb and press it. Keep the rest of your three fingers straight upwards.
- Sit in this posture for 10-15 minutes, and keep breathing slowly.
- Remove all thoughts from the mind and concentrate the mind only on Om.

Time to do Prithvi Mudra

Do this every day for 30-40 minutes. If you practice this every day, you will get good results. Practicing this mudra in the morning and evening is more fruitful.

Benefits of Prithvi Mudra

- It strengthens the bone system and muscles of the body. Therefore, Prithvi Mudra is very beneficial for weak children, women and persons. Increases the weight of weak people.
- Removes the deficiency of vitamins in the body, which increases our energy and brings glow on the face.
- Prithvi Mudra expands life force. Body is shapely. Helpful in increasing height and weight. It is very beneficial for growing weak children.
- Vitality, glow and radiance increases in the body.
- This posture gives a feeling of inner happiness. Generosity and thoughtfulness give happiness by making the goal bigger.
- Brings meaningful flow in the internal subtle elements. It reduces narrow-mindedness and makes us generous. Hence, it paves the way for spiritual progress.
- This posture improves digestion. People who have weak digestive power always look weak and tired. Many children eat a lot but still remain thin - if such children practice this mudra, it will be very beneficial.
- Due to increase in the energy power of the body, the brain also becomes more active – working capacity increases.
- Prithvi Mudra also protects from cold and cough.
- Like the thumb, the ring finger also has a special electric current, hence tilak is applied on the forehead with this finger.

- With continuous use of this mudra, there will be significant changes in your narrow thoughts. Along with your thoughts, your intensity and elemental qualities will also expand.
- Practicing this posture for a long time will have miraculous effects on the body. There will be new enthusiasm, new energy, joy and vigor in every pore of the body.
- Earth element is related to Mooladhar Chakra. Hence, with Prithvi Mudra, Muladhara Chakra gets activated and the organs associated with it get strengthened. The inflammation of the prostate gland ends. Hernia is cured and this posture is also beneficial for hair and nails.
- Children who are hyperactive are deficient in the earth element and more in the sky element. They should do Shunya Mudra and Prithvi Mudra together.
- Supply of vitamins/minerals keeps hair healthy. Hair fall stops and hair does not turn grey.
- This mudra is very beneficial for increasing hemoglobin.
- Removes lack of self-confidence.
- This posture maintains the ratio of components in the body.
- This posture relieves stress.
- Facial skin becomes clean and shiny.
- Prithvi Mudra strengthens the body internally and increases memory power.
- This is a beneficial Yoga Mudra for Weight Loss. With its help weight can be reduced.
- This posture helps in maintaining the body healthy.
- By doing Prithvi Mudra the throat becomes melodious.
- It is helpful in increasing concentration.
- Provides relief from mouth and stomach ulcers etc.

Necessary Precautions While Doing Prithvi Mudra

While doing Prithvi Mudra, sit in Padmasana and keep your spine straight. First do this mudra for 10-15 minutes every day, after a few days increase the time period. If you have Kapha dosha then do not do this posture for a long time. This mudra should be done on an empty stomach.

3.3 Special Instructions for Currencies

1. There are some mudras which are generally beneficial if practiced for at least 45 minutes throughout the day. These can also be done for longer periods of time as required. If any posture is done continuously for 45 minutes, the element changes.
2. There are some postures which have to be done for a short period of time - these have been described in the article about those postures.
3. The time limit for some postures is given up to 5-7 minutes. There is no harm in increasing this time limit by one or two minutes. But keep in mind that if there is any problem by applying any mudra for a long time, then remove the mudra immediately.
4. Gyaan Mudra, Praan Mudra, Apana Mudra can be done for a long time.
5. Some mudras have immediate effect like - Shoonya Mudra in ear pain, Apana Mudra/Apanavayu Mudra in stomach pain, Vayu Mudra/Apanavayu Mudra in angina. While doing such mudras, when the pain subsides, open the mudra immediately.
6. It becomes easier to practice the postures for a long period at night. While sleeping at night, make a posture and tie the tape, and whenever you wake up at night, remove the tape. Tape can be applied even during the day because continuous posture provides quick relief.
7. Although most of the mudras can be done anytime while walking, sitting or talking, but if the practice of mudras is done while sitting, with deep long breaths or

Anulom-Vilom, then the benefits are achieved very quickly.

8. It is better to apply tape in small children, weak persons and in emergency situations (for example, asthma, attack, paralysis etc.).
9. The posture of the right hand affects the left part of the body and the posture of the left hand affects the right part of the body. When there is disease in only one part of the body, then make the desired mudra with one hand and make Praan mudra with the other hand. Praan Mudra increases our vitality, and increases our immunity. But generally any posture should be made with both hands together.
10. Generally do not do any posture immediately after eating food. But after having food you can do Suryaa Mudra. Mudra can be performed immediately after meals only in case of emergency, such as ear pain, stomach pain, vomiting, asthma attack, etc.
11. If two or three postures are required simultaneously and there is paucity of time, then two postures can also be placed simultaneously. For example, do Suryaa Mudra and Vayu Mudra together, otherwise you can do Suryaa Mudra with one hand and Vayu Mudra with the other hand. In such a situation, change the hand postures after 15 minutes.
12. After doing one posture, another posture can be done immediately, but it should not be the opposite posture.

3.4 Benefits of Hand Mudras

1. Develops positive thinking about the body.
2. Brain, heart and lungs become healthy.
3. There is a lot of development in brain power.
4. This makes the skin shiny.
5. With its regular practice, the problem of gas, bile and phlegm goes away.

6. It is very beneficial in all mental diseases like madness, irritability, anger, restlessness, anxiety, fear, nervousness, insomnia, depression.
7. It is beneficial in all diseases related to air.
8. It is very helpful in reducing obesity.
9. Beneficial in heart disease and eyesight.
10. It also increases vitality.
11. It is beneficial in constipation and urination problems.
12. By practicing this regularly, one gets better sleep and also increases self-confidence.

Our body is made up of five elements and five sheaths, whatever is in the universe is in the body. The power to keep the body healthy lies in the body itself. Knowing this secret, the sages in Indian Yoga and Ayurveda told the people about the benefits of Yama, Niyama, Asana, Praanyama, Bandha and Mudra. Very few people would know the importance of one of these hand postures.

This body is made up of five elements – earth, water, fire, air and sky. There are five cells in the body such as Annamaya Kosha, Praanmaya Kosha, Manomaya Kosha, Vijnanamaya Kosha and Anandamaya Kosha. The body, mind and soul remain healthy only when these elements are in balance or the cells are healthy. Their imbalance or being unhealthy causes diseases in the body and mind. To make them balanced and healthy again, hand postures can be taken.

Ten (10) Hand Mudras:

Among the hand postures, the importance of ten major postures is as follows:

1.Gyaan Mudra, 2.Prithvi Mudra, 3.Varun Mudra, 4.Vayu Mudra, 5.Shunya Mudra, 6.Suryaa Mudra, 7.Praan Mudra, 8.Linga Mudra, 9.Apan Mudra, 10.Apan Vayu Mudra.

Other Strong Mudras

1.Surabhimudra, 2.Brahmamudra, 3.Abhayamudra, 4.Bhoomimudra, 5.Bhoomi Sparshamudra, 6. Dharmachakramudra, 7.Vajramudra, 8.Vitakamudra, 9. Jannamudra, 10. Karnamudra, 11. Sharanagatamudra, 12. Dhyanamudra, 13. Suchimudra, 14. Ommudra, 15. Janana Mudra, 16. Anguliya Mudra, 17. Mahatrika Mudra, 18. Kuber Mudra, 19. Chin Mudra, 20. Varada Mudra, 21. Makara Mudra, 22. Shankha Mudra, 23. Rudramudra, 24.Pushpaputamudra, 25.Vajramudra, 26.Shvas Mudra, 27.Hasya Buddha Mudra, 28.Yoga Mudra, 29.Ganesha Mudra, 30.Dynamic Mudra, 31.Matangi Mudra, 32.Garuda Mudra, 33.Kundalini Mudra, 34.Shiva Linga Mudra, 35.Brahma Mudra, 36.Mukul Mudra, 37.Maharshi Mudra, 38.Yoni Mudra, 39.Pushan Mudra, 40.Kaleshwar Mudra, 41.Esoteric Mudra, 42.Merudanda Mudra, 43.Hakini Mudra, 44.Lotus Mudra, 45.Digestion Mudra, 46.Detoxification Mudra, 47. Vipharan Mudra 48.Sky Mudra, 49.Heart Mudra, 50.Jaal Mudra etc.

The oldest text that tells about mudras and other yogasanas is Gheranda Samhita. This book of Hatha Yoga was written by Maharishi Gherand. There is mention of 25 mudras in Gherand and 10 mudras in Hatha Yoga Pradipika, but including the mudras of all the yoga texts, there are a total of 50 to 60 hasta (hand) mudras.

4.0 Some Special Mudras and Maha Asanas –Methods and its Benefits

4.1 Energy Walking Yoga Mudra – Obesity will go away

Obesity is a problem. Due to this, problems of stomach, back, waist and shoulders also persist. We are telling you the easiest way to remove obesity is Energy Chal Mudra Yoga. Actually this is part of organ operation (subtle exercise).

Benefits of Energy Moving Yoga Mudra

While this will strengthen your fingers, it will also prove helpful in reducing obesity. First of all it relieves shoulder pain and then it relieves stomach, back and waist pain.

Caution: Start with 5 minutes of practice and practice it every morning and evening for 10 to 15 minutes. Practice for up to 20 days and then leave two-four days and start practicing it again.

Do This Mudra Like This - it is very easy, knowingly or unknowingly you must have practiced it. For this you just have to close and open the fists of both your hands. This posture has to be done again and again. Doing this again and again is called Energy Chal Mudra.

4.2 Kaki Yoga Mudra – For digestion process

Kaak is called crow. Making a mouth posture like a crow's beak is called Kaaki Mudra.

Method of making the Kaki Mudra: Sitting in any posture, fold the lips like a thin tube and make them like a crow's beak. Now look at the front part of the nose and focus your entire attention on the nose. After this, slowly take a deep breath through the mouth and close the lips. After some time, exhale the breath through the nose. Do this for 10 minutes.

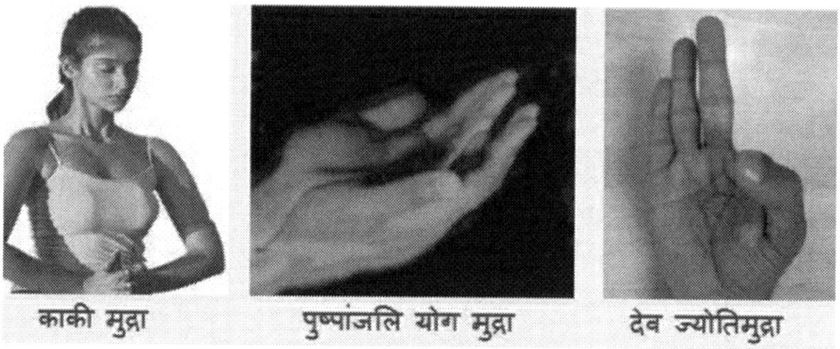

Figure-4.1: Specific yoga postures- a). Kaki Mudra, b). Pushpanjali Yoga Mudra and c). Dev Jyoti Mudra

Benefit of Kaki Yoga Mudra: While this Mudra increases coolness in the body, it is also beneficial in curing many diseases. By continuously practicing this mudra, the process of digesting food inside the body gets faster. This reduces the increase in acidity.

4.3 Matangini Yoga Mudra – For Youthfulness

Matang means cloud. Matangi is a form of Maa Durga. This is the ninth Vidya among the ten Mahavidyas. There is a meditation, mantra by the name Matang and the name of an elephant is also Matang. Matangi is also a name of sage Vashishtha's wife. Sage Kashyap's daughter's name is also Matangi from whom elephants were born. There are two types of Matangini Mudra –1.Matangini Kriya, 2.Matangini Hasta Mudra. Now Matangini Kriya is presented here –

Repetition period: This can be done repeatedly.

Method of doing the Matangini Mudra: In a quiet place, immerse the body up to the neck in water and then suck the water through the nose and take it out through the mouth.

Then pull the water out of the mouth and out through the nose. This action itself is called Matangini Mudra.

Benefits of Matangani Mudra: By practicing this mudra, eyesight becomes sharper. This mudra is considered very beneficial in headache. This also cures diseases like cold and cough etc. Continuous practice of this mudra brings glow on the face and hair also does not turn grey. When this posture is accomplished, the strength in the person increases.

4.4 Pushpanjali Yoga Mudra

As its name Pushpanjali proves, what type of currency this will be. This is an important hasta yoga mudra. This mudra is formed when we raise our hands in prayer or offer flowers.

Method of Doing Pushpanjali Yoga Mudra: First come into the Kapot Mudra i.e. join the fingers and thumbs of both the hands together and also join the Manibaddha. Then join the little fingers of both the hands together and make a shape like the one we make while offering flowers to a God, this is called Pushpanjali Mudra.

Benefits of This Mudra: Continuous practice of Pushpanjali Mudra helps in getting good sleep. Confidence increases.

4.5 Dev Jyotimudra Yoga – For Eyes

Making special shapes with the 10 fingers of the hands is called Hasta Mudra. All the five elements are present in all the fingers of the hands like fire element in the thumb, air element in the index finger, sky element in the middle finger, earth element in the ring finger and water element in the little finger.

For a person who is unable to do Yogasana and Praanyama, hand postures can prove useful, provided he does it regularly. Here is the introduction of 'Dev Jyoti Mudra' beneficial in eye diseases.

Method of Doing Mudra: Dev Jyoti Mudra is formed by bending the index finger of your hand and placing it at the root of the thumb. This is something like Vayu Mudra. Practice staying in this posture for about 40-60 seconds. You can do this four to six times in the morning and evening.

Benefits of This Mudra: Dev Jyoti Mudra has proved beneficial in all types of eye diseases. By doing this mudra, diseases like poor vision, cobwebs in the eyes and swelling etc. are cured. Children who have been wearing glasses at an early age can remove their glasses if they practice Dev Jyoti Mudra daily.

4.6 Hatha Yoga and Five Major Postures

Warning: This article is for information only. No one should try to do this after reading it, because it is only for seekers and not for common people.

There are five major postures described in Hatha Yoga to make the mouth, nose, eyes, ears and brain completely healthy and strong. Common people should practice the following postures only after learning from a knowledgeable yoga teacher. By the way, these mudras are only for the seekers who want to attain Siddhi by awakening Kundalini.

These five main mudras are- 1. Khechari (for mouth), 2. Bhuchari (for nose), 3. Chanchari (for eyes), 4. Agochari (for ears), 5. Unmani (for brain). Khechari tastes like nectar. Bhuchari establishes unity in the vital air. Chanchari improves eyesight and vision is visible. Through Agochari one experiences the inner sound and through Unmani the unity with God increases. Through all the above, control is established on all five senses.

4.6.1.Khechari: For this, the meat fiber connecting the tongue and the palate is slowly cut, that is, one whole barley is cut and left aside for a day. Then after three-four days a little more is cut. In this way, by cutting little by little, the blood veins of that place keep moving inwards. Along with biting the tongue, the practice of slowly pulling it outwards is done daily.

By practicing this, within a few months the tongue becomes so long that if it is turned upwards, it closes the breathing holes from within. Due to this, breathing is completely stopped at the time of Samadhi.

4.6.2.Bhuchari: Bhuchari Mudra relieves many types of physical and mental troubles. By the practice of Kumbhaka, the practice of raising the apana vayu and bringing it to the heart and mixing it with the Praan leads to Praanjaya (Praanjaya), the mind becomes stable and there is a possibility of the Praan contact rising up through the Sushumna path.

4.6.3.Chanchari: First of all, one should practice fixing the vision four fingers ahead of the nose. After this, fix the gaze at the tip of the nose, then practice fixing the gaze in the middle. By this the mind and soul become stable and the light is seen.

4.6.4.Agochari: One should practice listening to the sound within the body with the ears by completely concentrating the mind with all the senses on the sound within the body. This increases knowledge and memory and stabilizes the mind and senses.

4.6.5.Unmani: By practicing focusing the mind with complete concentration on Sahasrara (which is the place at the top of the head), the soul starts moving towards God and the person starts connecting with the consciousness of the universe.

Khechari Mudra gives Samadhi and Siddhi

Human tongue is of two types – long and short. The long tongue is called snake tongue. Due to the long tongue of some people, they can easily place it on the tip of their nostrils and do Khechari-Mudra. But the one who has a small tongue has to face problems. First of all they have to lengthen their tongue and for this they have to resort to friction and tapping. The nerve to which the tongue is attached from below has to be cut.

It may take a few years to perfect Khechari Mudra and the stimulation required for secretion of nectar. It also depends on the qualification of the person. There are some postures in yoga which only yogis do. Common people should not do these. Khechari Mudra is considered for seekers.

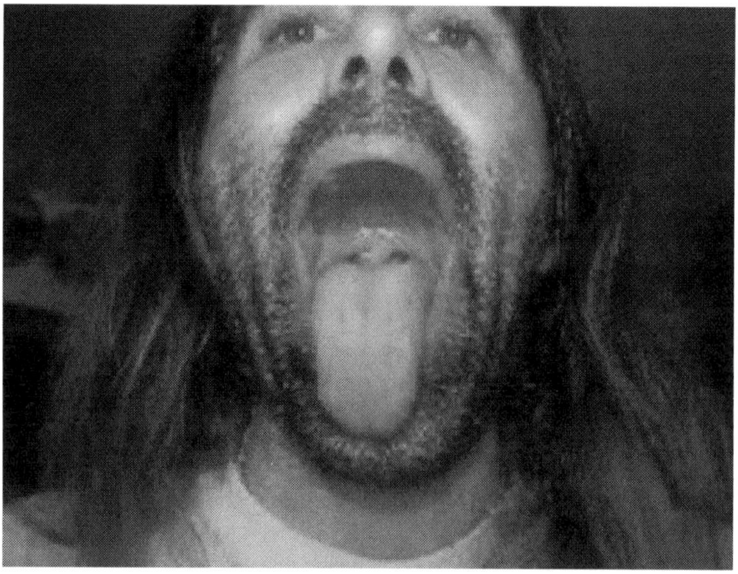

Figure-4.2: Khechari Yoga Mudra

Method: For this, the muscle tissue connecting the tongue and the palate is slowly cut, that is, a whole grain of barley is cut and left aside for a day. Then after three-four days a little more is cut. In this way, by cutting little by little, the blood veins of that place keep moving inwards. Along with biting the tongue, the practice of slowly pulling it outwards is done daily. By practicing this, within a few months the tongue becomes so long that if it is allowed to move upwards, it closes the breathing holes from within. Due to this, breathing is completely stopped at the time of Samadhi.

Benefits: This posture is especially helpful in perfecting Praanyama and attaining Samadhi. This posture is considered very beneficial for the sadhus during meditation.

Speciality: When the jib becomes long due to continuous practice, then it can be inserted into the nostrils. By meditating in this way, some glands related to the cranial passage and Bindu Visarga are stimulated. As a result of which secretion of nectar starts. When the same nectar is secreted, a special kind of spiritual experience occurs. This experience leads to rapid progress in Siddhi and Samadhi.

Warning: This article is for information only. No one should try to do this after reading it, because it is only for seekers and not for common people.

4.7 Mahamudra Asana

If you are troubled by your obesity and want to reduce extra fat and also increase your working power, then do Mahamudra Asana. Which will not only reduce your obesity but also provides energy to the body. Mahamudra should be done on an empty stomach after morning bath. Initially, it should be done 3-3 times with both legs, then keep increasing the number of Praanyam as per your capacity.

Method of doing Mahamudra Asana

- This asana is one of the asanas done while sitting. Many parts of the body are affected by the posture of Mahamudra.
- First of all spread the seat on the ground.
- Now sit on Asana with both legs spread.
- Keep the spine straight. Place hands on knees. Bend your left leg at the knee and bring the heel to your thigh.
- Keep the sole of the left foot touching the thigh. Raise your hands and breathe.
- Then touch your forehead to your right knee and hold the foot with your hands. This is the complete position of Mahamudra.
- Now exhale and stand straight. Straighten the right leg.
- Now come back to normal state. Practice this asana again by changing legs.

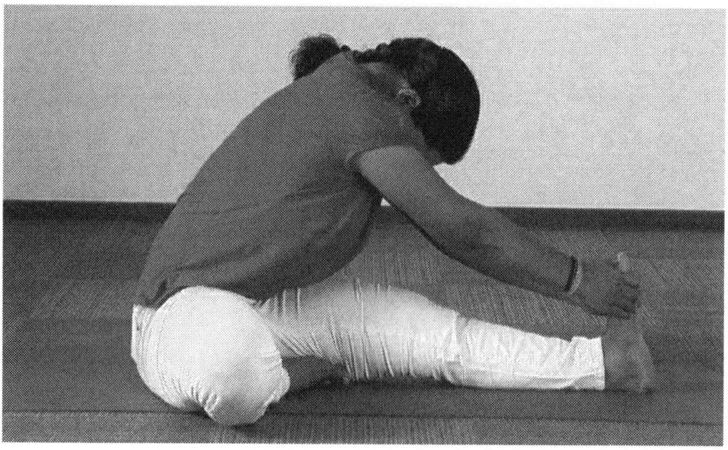

Figure-4.3: Mahamudra Asana

Benefits of Mahamudra Asana

- This asana is very beneficial in diseases like asthma, tuberculosis, leprosy, piles etc.

- Regular practice of this asana makes the stomach slim.
- Thigh area, spine, waist, shoulders and lungs become strong.
- Sushumna Nadi starts moving well.
- With this asana, the extra fat accumulated in the body starts getting removed.
- Pain in waist and legs goes away. This asana is very important in terms of benefits.
- This asana quickly removes the problem of nocturnal emission.
- This asana brings energy to the body.
- This asana is very useful for patients of diabetes and appendicitis.
- Laziness also goes away with its regular practice.
- By doing this asana, all stomach related diseases are cured.
- Women's problems related to menstruation go away.
- precautions
- A serious heart patient should not do Mahamudra.
- Those who have problem of slip disc (back pain) should not do Mahamudra.
- It is more beneficial to do Mahamudra on an empty stomach. Eat or drink something only after 30 minutes of doing this.
- Adopt yoga in your life, move towards a happy life.

4.7.1 Mahamudra Yoga

Mahamudra is described in all the texts of Hatha Yoga. Due to the importance of this posture it is called Mahamudra. This posture has a special contribution in awakening Kundalini.

Method of doing Mahamudra Yoga

The same method of Mahamudra is described in all the texts. It is said in Hathayoga Pradipika that -

"पादमुळें वामेन योनि सम्पीड्य दक्षिणम्।
प्रसारितं पदं कृत्वा कराभ्यां धारयेद् दृढम्।
कण्ठे बन्धं समारोप्य धारयेद्वायुमूर्ध्वतः॥"

Press the seam (the space between the anus and the intercartilaginous space) with the heel of the left foot, spread the right leg, hold the toes firmly with both hands, do Kumbhaka and apply Jalandhar Bandha and pull the air upwards.

"चन्द्राङ्गे तू समभ्यस्य सूर्याङ्गे पुनरभ्यसेत्।
यावत्तुल्या भवेत् संख्या ततो मुद्रा विसर्जयेत॥"

After practicing with Chandra Bhag i.e. left foot, practice with right foot also. Both sides should be practiced equally.

"पायुमुलं वामगुल्फे समपीडय दृढयत्नतः।
याम्यपादं प्रसार्याअथ करें धृतपदांगुलः।
कण्ठ संकोचनं कृत्वा भुरवोर्मध्य निरीक्षयेत।
महमुद्राभिधा मुद्रा कथ्यते चैव सुरिभिः॥"

Scholars call Mahamudra by pressing the inner region very firmly with the left heel, spreading the right leg and then holding all its fingers with both the hands, applying Jalandhara Bandha and observing the middle part of the eyebrows.

According to Grahyamal, the book of Hatha Yoga -
Press the vaginal opening with the heel of the left foot, spread the right leg, pull the chin into the throat (by tying Jalandhar), and after blocking the air through Kumbhaka Praanyama, do catharsis of that filled air slowly, never do catharsis rapidly. should do . This is called Mahamudra. Just as when a snake is punished with a stick, it becomes straight like a stick, in the same way Kundalini also becomes simple.

Benefits: Regarding the fruits of Mahamudra, it is said in Gheranda Samhita that –

"क्षयकासं गुदावर्त्त प्लीहाजीर्ण जवरंतथा।
नाशयेत सर्वरोगांश्च महामुद्रानिसेवनात।'

By practicing this mudra, all the diseases including tuberculosis, cough, anus, spleen, indigestion, fever are destroyed. It is said in Hathayogapradipika that –

"न है पथ्यमपथ्यं व रसाः सर्वेअपि निरसाः।
एपीआई भुक्तं विषं घोरं पियूषमिव जीर्यति।।'

For the seeker of Mahamudra, nothing remains edible or unhealthy. Even a dull thing becomes interesting. He easily digests even the most dangerous poison as if it were nectar.

"क्षयकुष्ठगुदावर्त्तगुल्माजीर्णपुरोगमाः।
तस्य दोषाः क्षयं यान्ति महामुद्रां तू योअभ्यसेत।।"

One who practices Mahamudra gets cured of diseases like tuberculosis, leprosy, constipation, flatulence, indigestion and many other possible defects.

Analysis:

Thus, it can be said that the practice of Mahamudra cures many diseases even at the physical level. Like, if the seeker does not have TB then he gets cured. Anal related diseases are cured. Metal becomes strong and urinary diseases also become exhausted. Any kind of blood impurity gets cured and gas formation in the stomach stops. The size of the spleen does not increase due to which spleen related diseases like fever due to cold, mild fever, shortness of breath are cured. Problems like constipation go away and indigestion does not remain.

Precautions:

- Practice only on an empty stomach.
- Apply Jalandhar Bandha completely.
- Do not practice if you have had any abdominal surgery.
- If there is excessive heat in the stomach, do light exercise.
- After Kumbhak, do catharsis slowly.

4.8 Mayuri Mudra

Yoga consists not only of asanas but also has many parts. Mudras are also a major part of yoga, and mudras have great importance in the practice of yoga. Regular practice of these postures removes old age and increases lifespan. It calms and concentrates the mind. Its specialty is that it also helps in doing other yogas.

Mudra is considered the third part of Hatha Yoga. The person who practices mudra easily controls his senses. Mayura Mudra is also a type of currency.

How to do Mayuri Mudra

In this posture the shape of the hand becomes like the head of a peacock, due to this it is called Mayuri Mudra. Mayura Mudra is ranked fifth among the 28 mudras that can be performed with one hand. To do this, first of all sit on the ground in any posture. After this, place the right hand on the knee and raise the left hand in front of the mouth. But keep the palm open and facing downwards. Place the thumb on the upper lip. Fix this hand together towards the smallest finger, that is, meditate on the empty space.

What are the benefits of Mayuri Mudra?

- It is very beneficial for the brain, regular practice of Mayuri Mudra sharpens the memory.

- By doing this mudra the mind also remains calm and negative thoughts do not come.
- This Mudra plays a very special role in Kundalini awakening.

Although this posture is very difficult to do, but with its continuous practice it becomes very easy.

4.9 Shambhavi Mahamudra

Among the mudras, Shambhavi Mudra is described in Bhagavad Gita, Patanjala Yoga Sutra, Amanska Yoga, Gheranda Samhita, Shashav Samhita, Goraksha Samhita, Hathayoga Pradipika, Yoga Chitamani and Abhinav Guptacharya and many other eternal scriptures of Yoga. Shambhavi Mudra is also called Adishakti Umaswarupani, Shivpriya, Shambhupriya etc. Mudra. It is clearly written in Swayam Bodh Amanasak Yoga that this knowledge is very secret and is accomplished only by a very rare virtuous soul.

The pictures that we see in Kriya Yoga of Lahiri Mahasaya and Avtaar Baba are in Shambhavi Mudra only. One can attain the state of liberation only by being in the company of a saint or Mahatma having Shambhavi Siddha Mudra and even just by having his darshan. Becoming knowledgeable about the past and future is a very simple thing for such Mahatmas.

Yoga and spiritualistic curious scientists of medical research have unanimously concluded that concentration, emotional balance, energy level in the body, mental peace and spiritual achievements along with allergies, asthma, heart diseases, diabetes, insomnia etc. Continuous practice of this mudra has shown miraculous benefits in many physical diseases like illness, depression etc.

The findings obtained from the EEG of Shambhavi Mudra practitioners revealed the fact that miraculously a balance is created between the left and right hemispheres of the brain and sharpens the intellect. If students or people whose work is related to education or other intellectual level are made to practice this mudra, then the results obtained from them will be even more satisfactory.

Method of Shambhavi Mudra

Sit in a meditation posture and keep your back straight. Your shoulders and hands should be in a completely loose state. After this, keep the hands on the knees in Chinmudra, Gyaan Mudra or Yoga Mudra. Concentrate your gaze on one point in front. After this try looking up. Make sure your head remains steady. Meanwhile, try to control your thoughts also. Just take care. Don't think about anything in the meantime.

During Shambhavi Mudra, your eyelids should not blink and yes, your gaze should not be fixed on one object, due to which there is a possibility of mind wandering. Do this asana for only a few seconds in the initial days. That is, as your ability to concentrate and control your thoughts improves, keep increasing the time limit for doing this asana. You can do this for maximum 3 to 6 minutes.

Benefits of Shambhavi Mudra

Shambhavi Mudra is a powerful kriya that awakens the Ajna Chakra. Let us tell you that Ajna Chakra is the center connecting lower and higher consciousness. Not only will you get physical benefits from this posture, this posture also strengthens the nerves of your eyes. Not only this, this posture keeps your mind and brain calm. That means, if you feel stressed due to something, you can reduce your stress with the help of this posture. As already mentioned, this posture is very special because under it the person is sleeping and enjoying meditation even with the eyes open. Through this yoga posture, you can also rid yourself of diseases like depression.

Caution

Yogacharyas always lay special emphasis on the fact that whatever yoga you do, do it only under the supervision of experts. Because timing and posture are very important in every yoga activity. Same is the case under Shambhavi Mudra also. However, this exercise is very simple and safe. Women and girls of every age group can do this. This yoga posture is very beneficial for men also. Despite this, take some caution while doing this asana. Do the things mentioned for Shambhavi Mudra slowly. Don't try to rush.

If you have any kind of physical problem and you feel pain while doing this posture, then do not do this asana. Keep in mind that it is appropriate to do this asana only after the age of 7 years. Do not force small girls to do this asana. Apart from this, do not do this posture while wearing glasses. And yes, if your stomach is not clean then you will not be able to concentrate in this asana. This means that before doing this exercise, clean your stomach so that you can concentrate well. If you do this posture under any yoga practice, it will be beneficial for you.

4.9.1 How to master Shambhavi Mudra

Sit in a simple, easy and pleasant posture in a peaceful, flat place. Keep your spine absolutely straight, at exactly 90 degrees relative to the flat place where you sit, and focus all your attention on the Ajna Chakra located between the eyebrows. There is nothing to be done, neither any mantra, nor any ritual, nor any chanting, penance etc. You just have to practice keeping your attention focused on this one place. One has to make such an effort that one should not pay attention to anything outside even with half-open or completely open eyes; one should become completely void of thoughts. One has to be so engrossed in meditation that no external object is visible. And this Kiya has to be understood as completely different from Tratak. It is written in Amansk Yoga that this Shambhavi Mudra is inward looking, outward looking and void of Nimesh-Unmesh. That is, in this posture, even if there is external vision, there is internal vision and there are no nimesha and unmesha in the vision.

In the initial stage during the practice, there is strain in the eyes and there may be pain in them, but gradually such a state starts arriving that even with closed, open or semi-open eyes, the attention is focused not only on the eyes but on some part of the physical body. The going stops. When seeing and meditating on external objects ends completely, then the seeker reaches a state of mind, life and pleasant sleep, separated from the object and the instinct of internalization. There is a difference between the earth and the sky between normal sleep and the sleep state of a Shambhavi seeker. In one case the mind reaches an unconscious state and in the other the mind remains conscious. He remains free from all worldly matters and from the mind attached to things. This is the supreme divine Shambhava element and this is a clear path to attain the eternal God. The practitioner who has mastered the Shambhavi Mudra becomes the embodiment of the Supreme Being.

4.9.2 Quit the habit of Smoking Cigarettes by doing Shambhavi Mahamudra.

Karthik was a happy chain smoker. The physical system of the young man had also maintained this habit well. But a day came when he no longer had the desire to smoke, why?

Came to know about inner engineering program from wife

She called me from the USA every day for seven days. Every day she told me how good she was feeling, what new she had learned, what else she understood about life. His enthusiasm and happiness were reaching me like a contagion, but it was the enthusiasm that comes from a yoga practice class. I thought, 'She will soon recover from these things.' Little did I know then how contagious yoga could be! After she finished her program, she started insisting to me that I should also become a part of that yoga program, *'Inner Engineering or Isha Yoga Program'*. Like any obedient husband, I tracked down a program in English that was going to be held in the coming month, in Anna Nagar, a few kilometers away from Nanganallur, where I live, in Chennai. As the days of the program approached, the same thing kept coming to my mind again and again, 'Why do I need to go there?'

All Attempts to Quit Smoking Failed

Ever since we got married, my relationship with my wife has been very good, I just have one habit that makes her restless from time to time. I was a chain smoker. Although initially I developed this habit due to social pressure, but gradually I got addicted to it. Soon drinking alcohol in the evening also became a part of it. I was young and exercised every day, so these things made no difference to my health. Yet the amount of time I was devoting to my physical exercise seemed to have no effect, except that it was working towards keeping my lungs and muscles in better shape.

On my wife's insistence, I tried several times to quit smoking, but all efforts were made with reluctance. No technique or resolution lasted more than a week. Well, now to make her happy I decided to participate in that yoga program. I had to devote just three hours a day for seven days. However, during those seven days, before and after each session, I smoked cigarettes continuously without any interruption. But gradually a change was coming.

I felt so much better after that exercise that I could not give up either the condition or the practice. Within a few days of practice, it seemed that smoking cigarettes was no longer enjoyable. Oh God! I didn't even want to leave him.

It was as if a war had broken out between Isha Yoga practice and my favorite cigar and I did not want to give up either of them. However, after forty days of practice, I came to such a state that I never felt like touching a cigarette again.

Soon I also gave up the habit of drinking alcohol. Now I don't even touch alcohol and I don't even know how this was possible. Today, when I look back, I realize how foolish it was to smoke cigarettes; after a few days, I did not get any intoxication from it. He was simply addicted to it, and as with every drug, he got satisfaction for a few moments after drinking it. Of course, the social company that came with it had made my mind a victim of this useless and harmful habit for health. I am lucky to have escaped its grip so easily. I found my addiction somewhere else. I salute those Gurus who handed over the treasure of Yoga to us.

Effect of 40 days practice of Shambhavi Mahamudra

In the beginning, the persistence of smoking decreased because if I had to practice twice a day, it was necessary that I not smoke a cigarette in the first four hours of practice.

Message to cigarette smokers

In conclusion, the message to smokers around the world is that if you smoke, don't quit. Continue your yoga practice continuously... Every useless thing stuck to you will disappear on its own, without leaving any trace. Then you can enjoy real life!

4.10 Siddhi Yoga Mudra

Tantra-Shastra is a very ancient spiritual system of India. Its specialty has been said to be that it does not prescribe difficult practices and harsh penances from the very beginning, rather, it gradually leads the mind inclined towards renunciation by steering it on the same path as a person's indulgence. From this point of view, Tantra was considered to be a means by taking the help of which even ordinary people can progress in the spiritual path. It is true that in the intervening period, the form of Tantra got distorted and it was mostly used to fulfill heinous purposes like killing, hypnotism, exaltation, subjugation etc., but the pure form of Tantra is not like this. Its main objective is to reach the pinnacle of self-improvement by climbing each ladder one by one.

4.10.1 Success of the Siddha Purusha

The life of a successful man is considered an ideal life. The one who failed, could not reach his designated place, has to face ridicule and regret. In this world only those who have achieved success are worshiped. People never get tired of praising him. The reason is that people expect from someone who has himself achieved success that he will be able to lead us on the path of success. People are afraid of coming in close contact with someone who has himself been defeated, has lost, has failed, they think that it might happen that due to association with this person we too may face failure and defeat.

Take a deep look at the lives of all the great men and famous people in the world. You will see that his successes were mainly helpful in raising him so high and making him famous. Even after achieving a small success in a small task, a person's courage increases and his courage quadruples. People's attention is drawn towards that success, they become his admirers, supporters and friends. A victorious person gets unexpected and unexpected support from others, as a result he moves rapidly on the path of success. The front keeps on winning and in the end the great man is called a man. On the contrary, the friends of a defeated and unsuccessful man also leave him, due to losing his courage, his hands and feet swell and gradually moving towards degradation, he finally falls into the abyss of darkness.

4.10.2 Achievement Through Prayer

It has been seen many times that by praying to God with a true heart, by requesting God to fulfill one's desired wish, that work gets completed. There is a spiritual secret to getting success from this prayer - that is that the person praying has the faith that-

1. God is so powerful that if He wishes, He can easily fulfill my wish.
2. God is merciful. Looking at his nature it can be expected that he will complete my work.
3. My demand is appropriate, necessary and justified, hence I will receive God's blessings.
4. I am praying with a true heart, attributing the best part of my conscience, faith, belief to God. Therefore my call will be heard.

Figure-4.4: Achievement through prayer

With the combination of these four facts, the petitioner's aspiration becomes stronger and he becomes confident of its fulfillment to a great extent and the light of the sun's rays becomes visible in his heart.

Having such a mental state is a prerequisite for success. Whatever may be the method, if a person makes his mental state such that there is full hope and full possibility of his wish being successful, then most of the time his wishes are fulfilled. Because due to the mood of hope and possibility, the physical and mental powers awaken exceptionally and the best measures have to be taken, paths are found and cooperation is obtained due to which the path to success becomes very easy and often it is also achieved. .

4.10.3 Siddhi through equality

By Pt. Tulsiram Ji Shastri, Vrindavan-

Equality – Having a feeling of intimacy and equality among all living beings is a very good spiritual quality. Equanimity is an essential element of human being, it should be used daily in personal life. Every system of equality should be spread in the social and economic fields also. Some verses of Padma Purana are given below. Seeing the extraordinary accomplishments of Tuladhar, Narottam had asked the Lord in Brahmin guise as to what was the reason for him having so many accomplishments? God told him that equality is the mother of all accomplishments. Libra has a strong balance and that is why it has achieved so many achievements.

सत्येन सम भावेन जितं तेन जगत्त्रयम्। तेनातृ प्यन्त पितरो देवा मुनि गणैः सह॥
भूत भव्य प्रवृ तं च तेन जानाति धार्मिकः। नास्ति सत्यात्परो धर्मो नानृ तात्पातकं परम्॥
विशेषे सम भावस्य पुरुषस्यानघस्य च। अरि मित्रेप्युदासीने मनोयस्य समं व्रजेत्॥
सर्व पाप क्षयस्तस्य विष्णु सायुँयताँ व्रजेत्।
समोधर्मः समः र्स्वगः समं हि परमं तपः॥ यस्यैव मानसे नित्यं समः स पुरुषोत्तमः।
विशेषे सर्व लोकेषु समो योगिष्वलोलुपः॥
एवं यो वर्तते नित्यं कुल कोटि समुद्धेरेत्। सत्यं दभः शमश्चैव धैर्यस्थैर्यमलोभता॥
अनार्श्चयमनालस्यं तस्मिन् सर्वं प्रतिष्ठितम्। नवै देव लोकस्य नर लोकस्य सर्वशः॥
जानाति धर्मज्ञस्तस्य देहे स्थितो हरिः। के तस्य समोनास्ति समः सत्यार्जविषु च॥

पद्मपुराण सृष्टि खण्ड अध्याय 47

Hey Brahman! That righteous Taladhar has conquered all the three worlds with truth and equality. Due to this his ancestors, gods and sages all remain happy. Due to these qualities he knows everything about the past and future. There is no religion greater than truth and no sin greater than untruth. The man who is free from sin and is stable in equanimity, whose mind is equal towards enemy, friend and indifferent, all his sins are destroyed and he attains the union of Lord Vishnu. Equality, religion and equality are the best penance. The person in whose heart equanimity always resides is the best among all the worlds, capable of being counted among the yogis and free from greed. One who always behaves equally in this way saves many of his generations. Truth, sensual control, mental control, patience, stability, greedlessness and lack of laziness are all qualities established in that man. Due to the influence of equanimity, a religious person comes to know the complete details of the world of gods and the world of humans. Lord Vishnu resides in person within his body. There is no one else in this world who can match him in qualities like truth and simplicity etc. He is the embodiment of Dharma and it is He who sustains this world.

Those who are devoted to duty, who have the power to do duty, do not look at anyone else. They do not look for opportunities, they only look at the situation and they make arrangements according to the gravity of the situation.

4.10.4 Ashta-Siddhi and Nava-Niddhi

a) Revelation of Brahma Vidya

Flying in the air, walking in water, making the body invisible or small or big, such achievements are described in some books but today they are not known. In search of such Siddhas, we have been traveling through difficult and inaccessible mountains, we have explored every nook and corner of India, we have met many secret, revealed, unknown and very famous Yogis closely and have the power to reach their bottom. I have tried my best, in my 20 years of continuous search, I have heard many legends, but I have not been able to see any such perfect man, who actually has the above mentioned Siddhis like flying in the air etc. Just as household jugglers perform amazing feats through their cleverness, hand skills and tricks. Similarly we have found many famous Siddhas performing miracles. When I got close to them after washing their loincloths for a long time, I came to know that in reality they do not have any true accomplishment, they are only proficient in the art of trapping people in their clutches through false actions. In such a situation, we cannot say anything definitely to the readers in this regard. We are writing these lines on the basis of personal experience; we cannot ask readers to believe anything about something that we have not experienced ourselves. It is possible that the existence of such siddhis has been written with exaggeration in some book, it is possible that there was some independent science to attain those siddhis which has now disappeared, it is possible that some hidden yogi with such siddhis is hidden somewhere and the world Couldn't know them yet. No matter how many guesses can be made regarding unknown and indirect things, it is not possible to say with certainty until there is some direct experience.

b). Patanjali Yoga Darshan

We cannot express our definite opinion about the siddhis described in Patanjali Yoga Darshan to readers like you. By increasing spiritual strength, many types of powers are obtained which everyone can experience directly. Information about *eight* Siddhis is as follows-

1. One who is interested in the spiritual realm, considers the soul to be different from the body and understands well the impermanence of worldly things, hence even after getting a few things, he goes about without grumbling and does not fear separation, loss, destruction, etc. There is no reason to be sad, three-fourth of the sadness is mental, one gets rid of it easily. People spend their whole life to get relief from sorrow, still they do not achieve the state of satisfaction, but through self-knowledge one attains it effortlessly, this is the first accomplishment.
2. When the intelligence of self-respect, love, harmony, honesty, service and help is awakened, one's behavior

towards others becomes very generous, polite and sweet, as a result, the behavior of others also becomes similarly sweet, helpful and pleasant towards themselves. Is . Due to increase in the number of friends, lovers, well-wishers and admirers, the mind remains filled with happiness and cheerfulness, this is the second Siddhi.

3. By identifying bad habits through introspection and trying to avoid them, mental peace is maintained, sins do not increase, due to purification of mind, the conscience remains light and various types of mental distractions do not arise and cause nervousness and restlessness. This is the third accomplishment.
4. Stability of mind has a huge impact on the body. Due to control of senses and calm mind, the body remains healthy and lives long, this is the fourth Siddhi.
5. Patience, courage, stability, tenacity, hard work increase with the increase of sattvik instincts, these increase innumerable types of abilities and difficult tasks become easy. This is the fifth Siddhi.
6. As the amount of humanity increases, everyone believes in him, people adopt the guidance, leadership and program of the believer, people become ready to take the biggest risks and sacrifice on the guarantee of his personality, without the state To rule is the sixth Siddhi.
7. Due to refinement of the intellect, one becomes capable of understanding the mood of others. The picture of the minds of others appears clearly on the pure intellect like a clean mirror. By understanding the hidden feelings of other people and behaving accordingly, one's work style becomes successful, profitable and beneficial, this is the seventh Siddhi.
8. Due to the purity of the soul, life is liberated, God is attained, and one resides in a state of true and happy bliss. Heaven and rebirth remain within the grasp, this

is the eighth Siddhi. The seekers of the spiritual path attain these eight siddhis in more or less quantity according to their spiritual practice. The happiness in search of which the extrovert people wander around making great efforts and yet remain disappointed, is many times more happiness than that which the spiritual seekers attain spontaneously. Are . Due to the influence of Ashta Siddhi, their life remains full of joy every moment, not even the shadow of sorrow can be seen near them.

Riddhis and Siddhis are meant to influence others. A wrestler enjoys independent happiness by increasing his physical strength, and at the same time causes harm and benefit to others due to the influence of that strength, similarly the Riddhis of spiritual wrestlers are Siddhis. With the power of Siddhis one makes oneself elevated, pure, peaceful, fearless and happy and with the power of Riddhis one causes harm and benefit to others. The nine Ridhis are as follows-

1. The emotion that is thrown at others with self-power is as powerful as an arrow. Both his blessings and curses are fruitful. The ancient stories of curses and blessings are not false, if an ascetic blesses someone with a true heart, then that person can be benefited and face trouble due to the curse, this is the first Riddhi.
2. Incurable and painful diseases can be cured by simple treatment of ascetic men. Due to the spiritual nectar mixed in their treatment, they can provide more benefits than even the top doctors, this is the second Riddhi.
3. The environment around the seekers is so strange and impressive that living in it brings about extraordinary changes in people. Bad and lax natured people change a lot by staying in the company of sages. Their physical and mental electricity is so strong that it does not leave

anyone who comes near them untouched without getting colored in their colors. This is the third Riddhi.

4. By means of mesmerism, hypnotism, parakaya entry etc., they can hypnotize a nearby or distant person and remove the mental defects from him and in their place, they can plant the seeds of virtues in his mind. This is the fourth Riddhi.
5. We can already see the kind of future that is being created as a result of past deeds. This is the fifth Riddhi.
6. The events and ideologies of the past do not get destroyed but remain imprinted in the God element. A spiritual seeker can see a person's past with his divine vision and can know the identity of a person without asking. This is the sixth Riddhi.
7. A Yoga practitioner can donate some part of his power, penance, age and ability to others and can take upon himself the sins and sufferings of others by his own strength. This is the seventh Riddhi.
8. A person with soul power can spread his ideologies invisibly with such tremendous influence that innumerable people have to bow before those ideas. You must have seen that the old preachers go around here and there using their tongues like clippers but they have no effect, but even if a true great man says a little, his powerful thoughts penetrate into the hearts of the most hardened people. They have such a strong influence that it becomes difficult to ignore them, great men with self-power can change the views of the public with their morale and can create a turning point. This is the eighth Riddhi.
9. Make the despondent hopeful, the lazy enterprising, the fool wise, the crying happy, the sinners virtuous, the poor prosperous, the destitute prosperous, the sleeping awakened, the man transformed into Narayana, Ardha Breathing life into the dead is the ninth Riddhi.

Yogis are naturally endowed with the eight Siddhi Nav Riddhis, one gets Riddhi Siddhis in the same amount as per his sadhana. It is bad to misuse them. By using it properly, spiritual strength increases. Where it is said to avoid them, it means not to misuse them or not to take interest in useless games of juggling out of curiosity. Yogi naturally gets Riddhi Siddhis, this is the natural order.

4.11 One - Siddhi of Flying in The Air

I Shivpriya, this part of the spiritual journey of Shivanshu ji, a close disciple of Guru ji, is beyond imagination; When I read it, I was surprised. Shivanshu ji has written many sadhana stories in his free book (e-book) and video series, which are waiting for editing and publishing permission from Guru ji. Whenever he gets time, Guru ji reads them and edits them. In the meantime, I got to read this treasure many times, which I am sharing with you.

Figure-4.4: Sadhu Flying in The Air

In one of his stories, he has written about what he saw in the eyes of a monk flying in the air. Sadhana Vidhan received from a Siddha Sadhu is also written. Besides, the scientific aspect of his meeting with Guruji has also been written in detail. I am sharing his story here in his own words for the inspiration of higher seekers. But be careful about one thing, even if it seems simple, do not adopt the method of Vayugamana Sadhana without the guidance of a competent Guru. This could prove to be very dangerous.

4.11.1 Shivanshu Ji's Story In His Own Words...

In those days there was a lot of confusion in my mind. Simply put, there was confusion. The reason for the confusion was lack of trust. Lack of confidence in yourself.

Had been participating in Guruvar's sadhanas for many years. Many miraculous experiences had taken place between Gurudev and his spiritual friends. I had seen from close quarters many such secrets of the spiritual world, which people cannot even think about.

There was a yearning in my mind that I too should achieve such a miraculous accomplishment. But the Guru was not allowing any such practice. Whenever he requested, he would do so without giving any reason; Would have postponed the matter. Because of this, I started thinking that perhaps I do not have the ability to do competent sadhanas.

Thinking about this, I was getting disoriented and confused. One day I insisted on doing a big meditation from my Guru. He remained thoughtful for some time, then said ok, get ready. With his permission I jumped with joy. Then the Guru said that there will be a condition.

I became calm, so much so that I could say I became sad. Because their conditions are not trivial. He said that for the sadhana for which I am sending you, you will have to remain normal after seeing the accomplished ones. I understood - in fact, I used to be amazed by seeing the miracles of accomplished people through my eyes. It became normal after a long time. Gurudev says- People who get amazed after seeing the results of their siddhis are of normal mind; Whereas a special state of mind is required for accomplishments. The things that seem special to ordinary people are common to accomplished people.

For a long time I was trying to keep myself normal even in surprising spiritual situations. I believed that now I was ready for it. So I told the Guru that I will not be surprised at all after seeing spiritual miracles. Gurudev took a full look at my face – smiled! As if I had said something childish. He said, get ready – you have to go to Darjeeling next week. I became happy. Applied for leave in the office. After 5 days I left for Darjeeling. I met a friend of Gurudev there. He was the owner of a hotel. He stayed in his hotel at night. By talking with him till late night, I acquired information about Darjeeling and the surrounding areas. The next afternoon the hotel manager took me out in his car. After walking for about two and a half hours, we went towards villages far away from Darjeeling. There a person wearing saffron clothes was found in a village. The hotel manager returned leaving me with him.

That person looked like a yogi. Bright on the face and shapely body, his name was Girdhar. He had an expensive mobile in his hand. Girdhar's gestures and gait reflected the richness of his values and his personality was very attractive.

From Girdhar's words it seemed that he knew Guruvar very well. He respected Gurudev a lot. Due to this, he was showing great affection towards me also. Within a short time we became acquainted with each other and began to feel like each other.

Girdhar was taking me towards the forests via footpaths. The roads were passable for several kilometers. People were coming there on bikes and cycles, yet Girdhar ji was taking me on foot.

The forest started ahead - one could go there only on foot - we kept walking. Darkness starts spreading quickly in the forests. We had gone only a few kilometers when the roads became invisible. Girdhar ji was probably aware of this, he took out two torches from his bag - gave one to me, then we started walking with the help of torches. Kept going for several hours. At one place on the way, a monk's hut was found. There was a monk and his two disciples in the hut, they knew Girdhar ji. We spent the night there and left early in the morning to move ahead. Girdhar ji told that he would reach in just a few hours.

I was not able to understand whether the forest was so long or whether we were wandering in roundabout ways. While walking, Girdhar ji looked towards the sky and bowed. My attention went there and I looked up. My eyes widened, I couldn't believe what I saw. My claim before the Guru was broken. I was amazed - I was surprised - I was amazed - My thinking was still normal. I could not reach the thinking of higher seekers. He is my Gurudev - Seeing me surprised, Girdhar ji said pointing towards the sky. Up there, a saint was flying in the air, my senses were blown away just by seeing him.

4.11.2 Know The Secret Of Naradji's Power To Fly In The Air...

ViGyaan Prasar (VP) - According to the report of the Department of Science and Technology, Government of India, a few years ago, the Archeology Department of China discovered some Sanskrit documents in Lhasa, Tibet and they were sent to the University of Chandigarh for translation.

The researcher there, Dr. Ruth Reyna, told that in these documents, the method of making the interstellar medium of the aircraft has been described. The interstellar medium is a mixture of hydrogen and helium particles, which is spread throughout the universe in a state of extremely low density.

He further explained that to operate the aircraft, anti-gravitational power is required and the anti-gravitational power system of 'Laghima' is analogous. Laghima is called Siddhi in Sanskrit and it is called levitation in English. According to Laghima Yoga, Siddhi is one of the eight Siddhis. As we see in our scriptures, Gods, sages and many deities used to travel by air. All of them used the same Laghima Shakti of anti-gravity.

The description and system of this Laghima Shakti (for planes) is found in the Chinese documents which are being translated. Levitation power is not a Tantric knowledge, but it is a power acquired through the practice of meditation. Actually it is a cosmic power, for which Yama, Niyama and penance-meditation are followed.

5.0

Yoga Bandha – Types and its Benefits

Yogabandh-Its literal meaning is 'knot', bond or lock. By practicing this, the Praan is tied to one part of the body. By practicing this, the Yogi successfully awakens the Kundalini by controlling the Praan. Both Bandha and Mudra are practiced together. The five major Bandhas are as follows –
1. Moolabandha, 2. Uddiyanabandha, 3. Jalandhara Bandha, 4. Bandhatraya and 5. Mahabandha.

Centralization of Praan takes place in the pelvic plexus through Mula Bandha, in the epigastric plexus through Uddiyana Bandha and in the carotid plexus through Jalandhara Bandha.

Moolabandha controls Apana Vayu, which performs the process of excretion. Uddiyana Bandha controls Sama Vayu which performs the absorption process. Jalandhara Bandha controls Udana Vayu which performs the process of swallowing food and separating the gross body from the subtle body. These Praans or vaya have been explained in detail in the book of author "Yoga Philosphy" in Praanyama. Bonds are a wonderful boon for humanity. These provide awakening of Kundalini Shakti, good health, long life, vigor, mental strength and many types of achievements. These cure many diseases of body and mind. These are the mysterious keys to open the inexhaustible stores of strength, inspiration and resolve.

5.1 Mool Bandha

Benefits and its Effects- Many benefits of Mool bandha have been described in yoga. By doing this mudra, constipation accumulated inside the body gets eliminated and appetite also increases. The heaviness of the body ends and lethargy disappears.

Beneficial in Sexual Diseases: Regular practice of this Bandha strengthens the sexual glands and provides relief in sexual diseases. This mudra is considered very beneficial in men's metal diseases and women's menstrual related diseases.

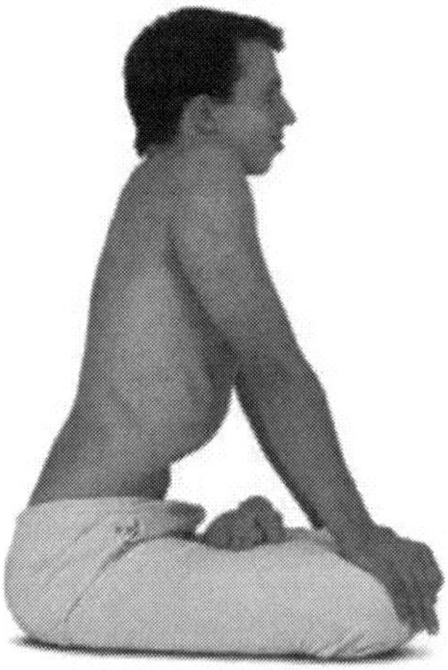

Figure-5.1: Method of Moolabandha Practices

Method to do Mool Bandha: Press the anus with the heel of the left foot, then sit in Siddhasana by placing the right foot on the thigh of the left foot. After this, practice pulling the air from below upwards while compressing the anus. In Siddhasana this work is done by the heel only.

While sitting in Siddhasana, both the knees should be touching the ground and the palms should rest on those knees. Then take a deep breath and hold the air inside. After this, shrink the anus completely. Now maintain the bandha for a comfortable period of time while holding the breath. In this position, keep Jalandhar Bandha also engaged, then leave the contraction of the perineum and slowly open Jalandhar Bandha and exhale slowly. Do this exercise 4 to 5 times.

Anal Contraction: To contract the anus and then release it. By doing this 15-20 times, all diseases related to the anus are cured. By doing this activity piles disease also gets cured. Its regular practice along with Moolabandha also increases lifespan.

Instructions- This Moolabandh should be practiced only under the guidance of a knowledgeable Yogacharya.

By using mudras and bandhas, dysentery, constipation, piles, cough, asthma, enlargement of spleen, vaginal diseases, leprosy and many other incurable diseases are cured. These are effective activities for celibacy. These are essential for spiritual progress. Moolabandha is described in the Gheranda Samhita as follows:

"पार्ष्णिना वाम पादस्य योनिमाकुचयेत्ततः ।
नाभिग्रंथि मेरूदंडे संपीड्य यत्नतः सुधीः ॥
मेढ्रं दक्षिणागुल्मे तु दृढ़बंध समाचरेत्।
जरा विनाशिनी मुद्रा मूलबंधो निगद्यते॥'

Compress the left heel of the cavernous region and firmly connect the umbilical cord to the spine. Again pull the navel inward and put it on the back and then connect the Upastha with the right heel firmly. This is called Moolabandha. This mudra destroys old age. The result of Moolabandha is given in the Gheranda Samhita as follows:

Those who want to cross the ocean of the world should practice this mudra secretly. Its practice definitely leads to great success. Therefore, the seeker should give up laziness and remain silent and meditate on it with effort.

In Matantar the Moolabandha is described as follows:

"पादमूलेन संपीड्य गुदमार्गं सुमंत्रितं।
बलादपानमाकृष्य क्रमादूर्द्धं समभ्येसेत्
कल्पितीय मूलबंधो जरामरण नाशनः।।'

By carefully compressing the Madhya Pradesh with the heel, Apana Vayu should be forcefully pulled upwards slowly. This is called Moolabandha. It destroys old age and death. Yonimudra is accomplished through this. Due to its effect the devotee can fly in the sky. By daily practice of Moolabandha, Apana Vayu is completely controlled. One gets relief from stomach diseases. There can be no semen disease. The seeker of Moolabandha experiences spiritual bliss without any conflict from a truly healthy body. Age increases. Its devotee also completes physical tasks with great enthusiasm. Among all the Bandhas, Moolabandha is the highest and extremely useful for the body.

5.2 Uddiyana Bandha

As we age, our skin starts becoming loose and our belly starts increasing. The rivers in our body through which blood flows also become weak. Everyone has to go through such problems, but when we do Uddiyana Bandha, it affects our increasing age. By doing this the person feels fresh and young. Due to this bandha, our eyes, ears, nose and mouth i.e. all our seven doors get closed. As a result of which Praan enters Sushumna and starts flying upwards. This is why we call it Uddiyana Bandha.

Method of Uddiyana Bandha

Uddiyana Bandha is a type of Bandha Yoga. Uddiyana Bandha is performed in two ways which are as follows-

Figure-5.2: Uddiyana Bandha practice **a).** Standing, and **b).** Sitting down

Standing Method

- First of all, keeping both your feet apart, bend both your knees and bend them slightly forward.
- Now place both your hands on your thighs and try to close all your seven pores by expelling the air from your mouth and pulling the navel inwards. This is your Uddiyan Bandha.
- Exhale and do external Kumbhaka for 20 to 30 seconds.

Sitting Method

- First of all, spread the carpet or blanket on a flat place.
- Then sit in Sukhasana or Padmasana.
- Place the palms of your hands on your knees and bend slightly forward, pulling the abdominal muscles inwards and do rechak, i.e. exhale your breath outwards.
- Now slowly inhale your breath and lift your ribs upwards.
- Hold your breath in your chest and leave your stomach loose.
- Shrink your stomach inward as much as possible.

This Bandha should be done on an empty stomach. In the beginning this should be done three times, later it can be done for more time.

5.3 Jalandhar Bandh

By doing this, blood circulation continues to operate smoothly in the nerves of the heart, brain and spinal cord. Jalandhar Bandha is a type of Bandha Yoga. There is a network of many vata nadis in our head, our body is operated through these, that is why it is very important for this part of our body to remain healthy and Jalandhar Bandha is a good solution for this. By doing this our head gets exercised and we remain healthy. Due to the effect of this Bandha, the nerves of sixteen places are affected which are as follows –

Penis, navel, heart, glans, glans, knees, thighs, seam, nostrils, cervix, throat, longbones, nostrils, eyebrows, skull, murdha and Brahmarandhra, all these places come under the influence of Jalandhar Bandha.

Method of Jalandhara Bandha

- To do Jalandhar Bandha, first spread a blanket or carpet on a flat ground and then sit in Padmasana position.
- Keep your body completely straight.
- Bend your neck in such a way that your throat and chin touch each other.
- Bend the head and neck so much that it touches the part of the chest below the chin bone and a gap of four to five fingers remains between the chin.
- In this action, the sequence of bringing your chin down and then raising it and straightening it should be followed.

- The sequence of inhaling and exhaling your breath should also be continued.

Figure-5.3: Method of Jalandhara Bandha Practice

Benefits of Jalandhar Bandha

- By its practice, transmission of Praan occurs in the right manner.
- Blood circulation starts happening properly in the muscles of our neck.
- Doing this brings strength in the mind.
- By doing this the blockage in the throat gets removed.
- By doing this, there is a stretch in the bones of our spine due to which our blood starts increasing rapidly.
- By doing this regularly, the functioning of our head, brain, eyes, nose etc. remains controlled.
- Can keep the arteries etc. of the body healthy.

Precautions

- Whenever you start this activity, Jalandhara Bandha should be applied by taking normal breathing.
- When you have pain in your throat or any kind of discomfort then you should not do it.
- One should not try to do this by force or coercion.
- You should not do this even when you have a cold.

5.4 Bandhatraya

Bandha Traya means three Bandhas or Tribandhasana. This yoga involves three important Bandhas, hence it is called Bandha Triad. These three Bandhas are – Uddiyana, Jalandhara and Moolabandha. These three Bandhas are practiced together.

Method of Bandhatraya Practice: Sitting in any Sukhasana, exhale and empty the lungs. Now while inhaling the breath, place the hands on the knees and forcefully do Moolabandha i.e. pull the anus upwards and pull the stomach inwards.

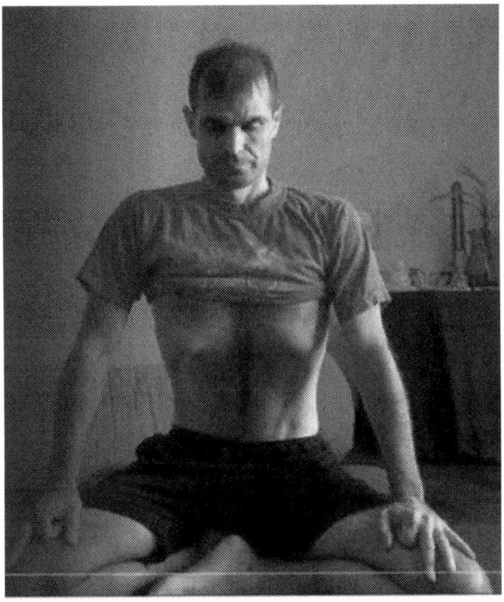

Figure-5.4: Method of Bandhatraya Practice

Then while exhaling, push the stomach towards the back as much as possible i.e. apply Uddiyana Bandha. Also apply Jalandhar Bandha by touching the chin to the throat.

Caution: Hold on to the above bandha position as per your capacity and then rest for some time. This yoga should be practiced in a clean and airy place. Do not do this Bandha if you have any serious disease in the stomach, lungs, anus and throat.

Its Benefits: It cures diseases related to throat, anus, urine, lungs and stomach. By its practice, diseases like: asthma, hyperacidity, dyspepsia, constipation, indigestion etc. are cured. This increases the glow of the face. Ulcerative colitis is cured and the efficiency of the heart also increases by removing contaminated air from the lungs.

5.5 Mahabandha

Take deep supplements and laxatives completely orally. Keep breathing out only. Place your hands on your knees, raise your shoulders and move your torso slightly forward while keeping your back straight. Do Jalandhar Bandha and concentrate on Vishuddhi Chakra. Perform Uddiyana Bandha and concentrate on Manipur Chakra. Finally come to Moolabandha and concentrate on Mooladhara Chakra. Maintain the three Bandhas, remain in this position for as long as you can easily hold your breath. Open the ties in the same order in which they were used. Inhale deeply and return to starting position. Remain in this position for some time with normal breathing.

Method of Practicing Mahabandha: First lift the right foot and press the seam firmly with its heel to close the anal passage. This is the state of Moolabandha. Then do Gomukhasana by placing the right foot on the left thigh and then place the chin firmly on the chest. This is the situation of

Jalandharbandh. Then keep your stomach pressed. Due to this the cold air flows upwards. During this time, concentrate on Trikuti. This complete situation is called Mahabandha.

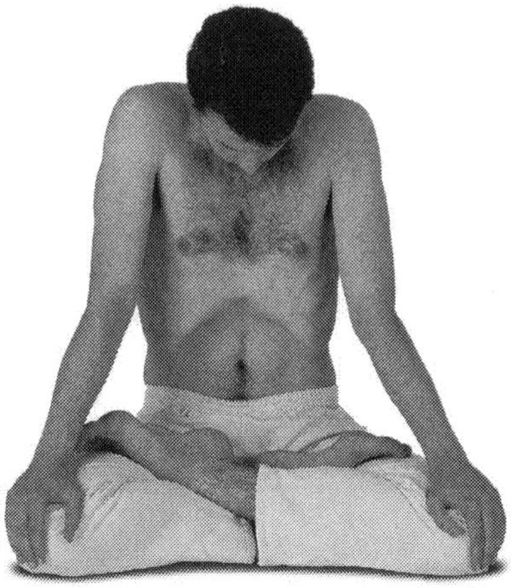

Figure-5.5: Method of Mahabandha Practice

Effects and Benefits: With its regular practice, the digestive fire increases, due to which the digestive power remains good. Old age and death etc. do not come near and the seeker becomes a yogi.

Duration and Caution: Do this every three hours. Do not consume women and fire (hot substances etc.) during practice.

6.0

Influence of Chakras in The Body

There are seven chakras or energy centers in our body through which our vital energy or life force flows. Sometimes, these energy channels become blocked and this leads to disease and disturbances in the body's natural processes. It is important to understand what each chakra represents and what we can do to keep this energy flowing freely. This is possible only when the chakras are balanced.

6.1 Balance of Seven Chakras Through Yoga Asanas and Mudras

When a chakra or wheel of energy becomes stuck, movement can help release the Praan (energy). Yoga mudras are a great way to release stale or stuck energy from the body as they invite fresh, vital energy back in through the posture and breath.

The practice of yoga ultimately leads us to a state of union, which is possible when we create a state in our body where energy flows freely from the base of the spine, the mool chakra, up to the head and beyond, can flow up to the crown chakra. When energy can flow freely through us like this, we can achieve a state of unity with the cosmic energy that flows through all living things. When each chakra is unblocked, it rotates like a wheel, hence the word 'chakra' means 'wheel' in Sanskrit.

Since yoga is both a physical and spiritual practice, yoga postures are exercises not only for your body but also for your mind, emotions, and spirit, making it an ideal practice for balancing your chakras.

6.2 Effect of Seven Chakras in The Body

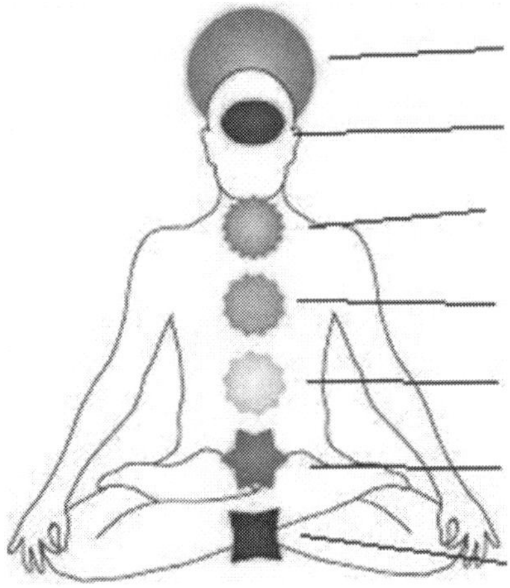

Figure-6.1: Location of Seven Chakras In The Body

Let us explore the seven chakras in our body, how they affect the body, what imbalances affect our personality and organs, and how to correct it by balancing the chakras with yoga asanas or postures.

1. Muladhara Chakra
2. Swadhisthana Chakra
3. Manipur Chakra
4. Anahata Chakra
5. Vishuddhi Chakra
6. Ajna Chakra
7. Sahasrara Chakra

6.2.1 Mooladhara Chakra

Element: Earth
Color: Red
Mantra: Lam
Location: Base of the spine between the anus and genitals

How Does it Affect The Body?
The Muladhara Chakra affects the health of the bones, teeth, nails, anus, prostate, adrenals, kidneys, lower digestive functions, excretory functions and sexual activities.

Symptoms of Unbalanced Muladhara Chakra:
Chakra imbalances lead to fatigue, poor sleep, lower back pain, sciatica, constipation, depression, immune disorders, obesity and eating disorders.

Practical Effect of Imbalance	Characteristics of Balanced Chakra
Baseless fear	Anger's sense of commitment and independence
Anger	Energy and vitality
Low self-esteem	Ability to digest food well
Insecurity	Strength and peace
Lack of ability to Digest Food properly	Ability to digest food well
Sense of Entitlement	,

Asanas That Balance The Chakras:
Grounding-in-feet poses like-

- Mountain Pose
- Side-angle pose
- Warrior pose
- Standing Forward Bend
- Bridge pose

6.2.2 Swadhisthana Chakra

Element: Water
Color: Orange
Mantra: Vaam
Location: Located at the base of the pubis between the genitals and the sacral nerve plexus

How does it affect the body:
The Swadhisthana Chakra is related to the individual's emotional identity, creativity, desire, pleasure and self-satisfaction, reproduction and personal relationships. It controls the sexual organs, stomach, upper intestines, liver, gallbladder, kidneys, pancreas, adrenal glands, spleen, central spine and the autoimmune system.

Symptoms of Unbalanced Swadhisthana Chakra:
An imbalanced Svadhisthana chakra leads to lower back pain, sciatica, decreased libido, pelvic pain, urinary problems, poor digestion, reduced resistance to infections and viruses, fatigue, hormonal imbalance and menstrual problems.

Behavioral effects of imbalance:	Characteristics of a balanced cycle:
Irritability	Feelings of compassion and friendship
Shyness	Spontaneity

Guilty feeling	Power of life
Tendency to blame	A sense of belonging
Sexual passion	Good sense of humor
Lack of creativity	,

Asanas That Balance The Chakras:

Hip opening poses like-

- Standing Wide Forward Bend
- Lean forward while sitting
- Wide angle pose

6.2.3. Manipur Chakra

Element: Fire
Color: Yellow
Mantra: Ram
Location: At the level of the navel in line with the gastric or solar plexus

How does it affect the body:

Manipura Chakra is related to the sense of belonging, mental understanding of emotions and defines self-esteem in a person. It regulates the effective functioning of the upper stomach, gallbladder, liver, central spine, kidneys, adrenals, small intestines and stomach.

Symptoms of unbalanced Manipura Chakra:

An unbalanced Manipura Chakra can lead to diabetes, pancreatitis, adrenal imbalance, arthritis, stomach diseases, stomach ulcers, intestinal tumors, anorexia/bulimia or low blood pressure.

Behavioral Effects Of Imbalance:	Characteristics Of A Balanced Cycle:
Lack of Self-Esteem	Energetic and Confident Nature
Sneaky Mind	Intelligence
Feeling of Depression	High Productivity
Fear of Rejection	Better Focus
Better Focus	Better Digestion
Inability to Take Decisions	,
Judgment and Short Temper	,

Asanas that balance the chakras-

- Suryaa Namaskar Mudra
- Warrior pose
- Backbends like Bow Pose or Dhanurasana
- Twists like sitting half-spinal twist
- Boat pose or Naukasana – like abdominal strengthening poses

6.2. 4. Anahata Chakra

Element: Air

Color: Green or Pink
Mantra: Yama
Location: At the cardiac plexus in the heart area

How does it affect the body:
The Anahata Chakra influences a person's social identity and influences traits such as trust, forgiveness, unconditional love, wisdom, compassion and soul issues. It is related to the functioning of the heart, rib cage, blood, circulatory system, lungs and diaphragm, thymus gland, breast, esophagus, shoulder, arm, hand.

Symptoms of unbalanced Anahata Chakra:
Imbalances can cause issues related to the thoracic spine, upper back and shoulder problems, asthma, heart conditions, shallow breathing and lung diseases.

Behavioral effects of imbalance:	Characteristics of a balanced cycle:
Difficulty with love	Feeling of completeness and completeness
Lack of hope, compassion and confidence	Compassion
Disappointment	Feeling of sympathy
Mood swings	Friendship
,	Optimism
,	Increased motivation
,	Outgoing nature

Asanas That Balance The Chakras:

Chest openers like -

- Camel pose
- Cobra pose

- Fish pose
- Praanyama such as alternate nostril breathing or breathing-Nadishodhana

6.2. 5. Vishuddhi Chakra

Element: Sound or Ether
Color: Blue
Mantra: Ham
Location: Nerve plexus of the pharyngeal area, at the level of the throat

How Does It Affect The Body?

Vishuddhi Chakra is related to personality traits such as communication, creativity, trust, truthfulness, self-awareness and expression. It controls the throat, thyroid, and parathyroid glands, trachea, cervical vertebrae, vocal cords, neck and shoulders, arms, hands, esophagus, mouth, teeth, and gums.

Symptoms of unbalanced Vishuddhi Chakra:

Imbalance of the Vishuddha Chakra causes thyroid disorders, sore throat, stiff neck, mouth ulcers, gum or teeth problems, laryngitis and hearing problems.

Behavioral effects of imbalance:	Characteristics of a balanced cycle:
Disbelief	Increase creativity and

	expression
Indecision	Effective communication skills
Weak will power satisfaction	Satisfaction
Lack of expression	Good hearing ability
Lack of creativity	,
Propensity for addiction	,

Asanas that balance the chakras:

- Fish pose
- cat stretch
- Neck stretches like Balasana and Supported Shoulder Stand
- Bridge pose
- Plow Mudra

6.2.6. Ajna Chakra

Element: Light
Colour: Indigo
Mantra: Om
Location: Between the eyebrows (third eye)

How Does It Affect The Body?

Ajna Chakra is related to self-awareness, knowledge, intelligence, foresight, implementation of ideas, detachment, insight, understanding and intuitive reasoning. It controls the functions of the brain, eyes, ears, nose, pituitary gland, pineal glands and nervous system.

Symptoms of unbalanced Ajna Chakra:
Any imbalance can lead to headaches, nightmares, eye strain, learning disabilities, anxiety, depression, blindness, deafness, seizures or spinal cord damage.

Behavioral effect of imbalance:	**Characteristics of a balanced cycle**
Poor Judgment	Clear Thinking
Confusion	Healthy Imagination
Fear Of Truth	Strong Intuitive Power
Concentration Issues	Improve Focus
Propensity For Addiction	Characteristics Of A Balanced Cycle

Asanas that balance the chakras:

- Child's pose
- Attention
- Sitting Yoga Pose
- Eye exercises such as eye tapping and rotational viewing

6.2. 7. Sahasrara Chakra

Element: Prudence
Color: Purple or white

Mantra: silence
Location: Crown of Head

How does it affect the body?
The Sahasrara Chakra influences intuitive knowledge, connection to spirituality, mind-body-spirit integration and conscious awareness. It controls the center of the head and the midline above the ears, brain, nervous system and pineal gland.

Symptoms of unbalanced Ajna Chakra:
An imbalance in the Sahasrara Chakra causes chronic fatigue and sensitivity to light and sound.

Behavioral effects of imbalance:	Characteristics of a balanced cycle:
Lack of purpose	Feeling of oneness with the universe
Identity crisis	Open mind
Disbelief in any spiritual practice, or devotion	Intelligence
Lack of motivation	Thoughtfulness
Feeling of fear	Receptivity to thoughts and ideas
Materialistic nature	An overall harmonious personality

Asanas That Balance The Chakras:

- Balancing poses like Tree Pose that bring body awareness
- Yoga posture
- Attention
- Imbalance is a part of life, however, regular practice of yoga asanas will help you balance your chakras,

allowing you to live a full, satisfied and happy life in the pink of health!

6.3 Method of Opening and Balancing The Chakras

A chakra or a wheel is a point of Praan (energy) in our subtle body, located in the physical counterparts of our body such as veins, arteries and nerves. Whenever Praan or life force gets blocked then Yoga is a very beneficial way to free it. Yoga releases rotten and foul energy and invites fresh energy into our system through postures and breathing.

Each of the seven chakras has its own consciousness and is related to our emotional well-being. The Muladhara or Root Chakra is located at the base of the spine and is related to basic human instincts and survival. The Swadhisthana chakra is located on the sacrum above the root chakra and is analogous to the reproductive chakra. Above this, the Manipura Chakra is located in the abdominal region and is related to self-esteem, power, fear etc. and physically it is related to digestion. Above this, the Anahata Chakra is located in the chest slightly above the heart and is associated with love, inner peace and devotion. Next is the Vishuddhi Chakra, located in the throat and associated with communication, self-expression etc. Above this is the Ajna Chakra, which is located between the eyebrows and responds to intuition, imagination and the ability to deal with situations. Finally, there is Sahasrara, which is at the top of the head and is associated with inner and outer beauty, connection with spirituality.

When yoga and mudra are practiced, the chakras become balanced and enable our systems to function in a stable, balanced manner, both physically and emotionally.

6.3.1 Some yoga asanas to balance the chakras include:

- **Tadasana (Mountain Pose):** Enhances your connection to the earth, connecting you to your body and grounding you in the present moment.

- **Virabhadrasana (Warrior Pose):** This is a powerful posture that creates a strong connection between the earth and your body. This yoga pose mobilizes your Praan throughout your body, strengthening the first chakra. It physically strengthens your legs, opens your hips and can help provide knee and lower back strength.
- **Setubandhasana (Bridge Pose):** This is an energizing root chakra yoga pose that plants your feet firmly in the earth and stretches your spine to release a tremendous amount of Muladhara chakra energy. Sethumudra also stimulates the throat chakra, opens the heart and solar plexus chakras, and balances the sacral chakra.

6.3.2 Some postures also help in releasing Praan and opening the chakras. They include:

• To awaken Muladhara Chakra

1. Sit comfortably, keep your spine straight and focus your attention on your perineum, the space between the anus and the genitals.
2. Make a circle with your index finger and thumb. Rest your hands with your palms facing the sky on your knees.
3. Take a deep breath and exhale.
4. Repeat for 7 to 10 breaths.

• To awaken the Swadhisthana Chakra

1. Rest your right hand on your left hand in your lap, palms facing the sky, both sit comfortably. Keep your spine straight and focus your attention from an area one inch below your navel. Center up to the first lumbar vertebra.
2. The thumbs should lightly touch each other.
3. Take a deep breath and exhale.
4. Repeat for 7 to 10 breaths.

- **To awaken the Manipur Chakra**
  1. Sit comfortably, keep your spine straight and focus your attention from your navel to the solar plexus and eighth thoracic vertebra.
  2. Keep your fingers straight, facing forward and touching each other at the top. Make a 'V' shape with your thumbs. The right thumb should remain crossing the left thumb.
  3. Take a deep breath and exhale.
  4. Repeat for 7 to 10 breaths.

- **To awaken the Manipur Chakra**
  1. Sit comfortably, keep your spine straight and focus your attention from your navel to the solar plexus and eighth thoracic vertebra.
  2. Keep your fingers straight, facing forward and touching each other at the top. Make a 'V' shape with your thumbs. The right thumb should remain crossing the left thumb.
  3. Take a deep breath and exhale.
  4. Repeat for 7 to 10 breaths.

- **To awaken Anahata Chakra**
  1. Sit comfortably with your spine straight and focus your attention from your heart area to the first thoracic vertebra.
  2. Make a circle with your index finger and thumb. Rest the palm of your left hand on your left knee. Raise your right hand to between your breasts, palm slightly tilted toward your heart.
  3. Take a deep breath and exhale.
  4. Repeat for 7 to 10 breaths.

- **To awaken Vishuddhi Chakra**
  1. Sit comfortably, keep your spine straight and focus your attention from the base of the neck to the third cervical vertebra.
  2. Make a circle with both your thumbs touching and cross your fingers together and make a loose cup shape. Raise your hands to the front of your throat, solar plexus, or let them rest in your lap.
  3. Take a deep breath and exhale.
  4. Repeat for 7 to 10 breaths.

- **To awaken the Ajna Chakra**
  1. Sit comfortably, keep your spine straight and focus your attention on your third eye area, starting from slightly above the point between the eyebrows and extending up to the first cervical vertebra, encompassing the interior of the skull. .
  2. Make the shape of a heart by touching the ends of both your thumbs and index fingers, and let your ring and pinky fingers touch each other. Make a crown with the middle fingers. Raise your hands and place them in front of the third eye, solar plexus, or let them rest in your lap.
  3. Take a deep breath and exhale.
  4. Repeat for 7 to 10 breaths.

- **To awaken the Sahasrara Chakra**
  1. Sit comfortably with your spine straight and focus your attention on your crown area located at the top of your head and about three inches above your skull.
  2. Clasp the hands by crossing the fingers inwards and placing the left thumb below the right one. Raise both the ring fingers and form a crown. Raise both

arms above your head, resting in front of the solar plexus, or in your lap.

3. Take a deep breath and exhale.
4. Repeat for 7 to 10 breaths.

Along with a daily yoga practice, postures, meditation and breathing exercises help to open these chakras, which can have a positive and intense effect on our body, mind and spirit.

7.0 How To Make Life Happy?

We know very well that air-conditioned rooms or railway compartments are made so that the people working or living in them do not face unnecessary pressure of cold and heat. Excitement, whether due to season or any other reason, is tolerated only to a certain extent. Even in extreme situations, one can somehow live but one cannot work as enthusiastically as one should. Restlessness always surprises.

Restlessness is not only due to season but also due to other reasons. When the temperature increases, fever increases and in cold disease the natural temperature of the body decreases. Excessive rise or fall of blood pressure is also a disaster. Similarly, getting overwhelmed by anger or feeling disappointed due to depression is such a situation in which a person becomes unbalanced. Which is also called stress. There are two types of stress, one emotional and the other depressive. A state like anger is called anger and disappointment and passivity are called depression. Both the imbalances disturb the physical and mental health of the person and create such an unnatural situation in which nothing gets done by thinking or understanding. Such patients are considered to be a type of patients who are surprised by themselves and also surprise the people they come in contact with.

Maintaining balance is like living in an air-conditioned house in which a person remains relatively happy and content. The proportion and level of work also increases in happiness.

The structure of the world is like this. The sequence of circumstances moves like the ebb and flow. Sometimes favor comes and sometimes one has to face adversity. On such occasions, light, shallow, petty, childish people get uprooted, but those who are heavy remain fixed on their place like a rock. They keep looking at the ups and downs from the perspective of a player, in which sometimes one has to win and sometimes one has to lose.

Dissatisfaction is such a disease that it is not visible directly but it twists us from within. This affects not only health but also activities. They become disoriented. If thinking and doing is not done mindfully then it cannot be expected to be right. One who is disturbed in mind will remain ill, if not today or tomorrow.

It is not possible for circumstances to remain favorable all the time. When there is a period of change everywhere in the world, it is futile to hope that adaptability will remain constant. It is possible that if you have to walk on a thorny path, you should make arrangements for shoes and if the sun is shining brightly, you should carry an umbrella. Before disturbing our mental state, we should practice such that we can protect ourselves when the time comes.

The first practice is to relax to reduce the pressure of an inappropriate situation. This sadhana reduces half-sleep and reduces fatigue. Thus, freedom from worries is achieved only when one gets deep sleep or death takes away from this world.

Relaxation should also be included in our daily exercises and yoga practices. The process of making the body relaxed and the mind drowsy is not difficult. Lying on a soft bed and feeling as light as cotton or feeling drowsy, with a few days of practice this situation can be achieved and with the help of will power, you can take yourself to a semi-sleep state.

The second practice is to concentrate the mind, speech and body on one task. These three major powers should not be allowed to disintegrate. Everyone tells the glory of concentration and also suggests its use, but the simplest and most useful way is to consider the work in front as the most important and to make it a matter of prestige to do it properly. The one who works with all his heart and with all his hard work, his speech also does not talk nonsense. In scattering the powers, nonsense here and there is also a big vice. Due to this every work remains incomplete. Just as silence is maintained at the time of meal or worship, in the same way one should be prompt and focused in every small and big task and one should control one's talkativeness.

Many times man's intolerance and extremism turn a molehill into a molehill and a small difficulty, loss or failure turns a mountain out of a molehill and leaves a man distressed. The cure for that problem is to develop the habit of always laughing and smiling. Smile is the greatest cosmetic. As soon as we adopt this, even the ugly starts looking beautiful. The burden on the mind goes away. Living a light, cheerful life is a high level artistry. By including this in your daily practice, you should make yourself accustomed to being carefree and free from conflict. Minimum importance should be given to ups and downs.

Some people suffer from bad thoughts, evil deeds and mental diseases. As a result, they have to face non-cooperation and insult at every step. It is appropriate for such people to think about the excellence of qualities, actions and nature of successful people and try to mold themselves in the same mold. When the process of introspection for self-improvement begins, the personality begins to shine and improve. A person who cultivates decency in his qualities, actions and nature is generally a manasvi. Remains satisfied and gets respect.

Some people are very busy in greed and attachment and are so engrossed in the obsession of making grandeur that they forget spiritual needs and human dignity and contemporary duties. Such people should practice the separation of soul and body.

As soon as one wakes up in the morning, one should feel like one has got the life of a child and at the same time one should think on what conditions one has received this supremely important artwork of the Creator. What is the nature, goal and proper use of life? On the basis of this conclusion, such a routine should be made in which apart from the physical journey, the divine desire of soul's upliftment and inclination towards public welfare is fulfilled.

While sleeping at night, one should consider sleep as a rehearsal of death and think that the mistakes made today in the form of favoritism towards the body and injustice towards the soul will not be allowed to happen in the future. The definite effect of this evening worship is that the misuse of life's wealth is curbed and efforts are made to make life meaningful.

Every day, at a convenient time, one should seriously think about the four subjects of self-introspection, self-protection, self-construction and self-development and make a plan to move forward in the material field and rise higher in the spiritual field.

Works favoring greatness are not accomplished because most of the power gets drained through the holes of incontinence and there is no capacity left to do anything great. It is necessary that constant attention should be paid to restraint of senses, restraint of money, restraint of time and restraint of thoughts and in this way, the remaining wealth should be used in those works which serve both the purposes of self-welfare and public welfare. This is the process of making life conditioned.

7.1 Health benefits of yoga

Even if you are not in the habit of exercising, you can practice yoga. You may not be as flexible as the next person, but you'll get there. Yoga is always a work in progress and never a competition. While it is a physical practice, yoga will inevitably touch on your spiritual side. It unites mind and body to become one.

Yoga will not bring untold wealth, although the material benefits are notable. The world is already filled with abundance, much of which we ignore. The real beauty of yoga is that it prepares us for the present, connecting us to the abundance that is within our grasp. A better, more fulfilling life is within our reach when we let go and simply accept what it is.

Research conducted during the 20th century has found countless physical benefits of practicing yoga.

Stress Relief

Our lives are full of daily stresses, and we know that stress can happen. Causes tremendous harm to body and mind. The boss wants to talk, your spouse is upset, the mortgage is overdue, that means the mortgage is overdue and annoying kids.

Doing yoga asanas, stretching muscles, focusing on gifts and breathing deeply and slowly helps us achieve a state of greater relaxation and harmony. We are able to consciously choose our response to stress, rather than being at the mercy of it.

Staying calm in difficult situations is a choice, and yoga can provide the tools.

Yoga and Pain Relief

Studies have proven that practicing yoga can provide tremendous relief to people suffering from multiple sclerosis, arthritis and other chronic conditions. We will discuss its amazing effects on the auto-immune system and cardio system in more detail in other chapters.

Yoga and Breathing

Yoga combines physical movements with breathing. Slow, deep breathing can reduce stress.

Yoga and Flexibility

Yoga involves a lot of stretching, which strengthens the muscles. Since yoga affects the entire body, flexibility and elasticity from head to toe. It also loosens tight, tense muscles and helps us relax more.

Yoga and Weight Management

Doing yoga does not burn as many calories as some other exercise methods. However, it increases body awareness. People who practice yoga become more aware of what they eat and what are the effects? Such food affects their health and reduces unwanted weight.

Yoga and Circulation

If your blood is not properly supplying oxygen to your body and brain, your health will suffer. You need proper circulation for brain function, energy and cell growth. Sluggish circulation can cause nerve and tissue damage, blood clots, dizziness, among other problems. Doing thorough stretching in most yoga poses will improve circulation. Camel currency in this is a great way to improve circulation.

Yoga and Cardio Fitness

For patients who have experienced heart surgery, depression and anxiety can be natural consequences. Yoga can be helpful in managing this type of post-operative stress. It may also lower blood pressure, acting as a preventive heart-healthy measure.

There Is No Rush – Take Your Time In Yoga

It will take time to reap the various benefits. Yoga is not a two-week miracle program. So, as you begin with your yoga sessions, allow enough time for the results to manifest themselves. By doing this you will see a big difference in about two months. Whatever your situation, focus should be on improving all aspects of your yoga practice and how you do it.

7.2 Controlling Diabetes (Blood Glucose) Levels

To control diabetes/sugar (blood glucose) level it is necessary to follow simple Praanyams and asanas. After studies in top universities of western countries, it has been confirmed that along with ancient science, Yoga has a positive effect on health and it has been widely propagated there. Although this is the ancient heritage of India which now the whole world is forced to adopt.

Studies have also confirmed that Dhanusasana (Bow Pose), Vakrasana (Bending Pose), Matsyendrasana (Half Spine Pose), Halasana (Plough Pose) squeeze and compress the abdomen, Ardha Matsyendrasana (Half Twist Pose) and Practicing certain asanas like Mandukasana and helps in stimulating pancreatic secretion or hormonal secretion. As a result, more insulin is pushed into the system. It rejuvenates insulin producing beta cells in the pancreas of diabetics suffering from both type 1 and 2 diabetes. Practicing the postures comfortably without any exertion, meditation and breathing techniques helps most of the patients to control the triggers or causes of diabetes.

7.2.1 Dhanurasana

This asana got its name because of its bowed shape. Dhanurasana is one of the asanas in the category of Padma Sadhana. This is properly known as Dhanu-asana.

Dhanurasana = bow + asana

Figure-7.1: Method of doing Dhanurasana

How to do Dhanurasana?

- Lying on the stomach, keep the feet as far apart as the buttocks and keep both hands straight on either side of the body.
- Bend the knees and bring them near the waist and hold the knees with hands.
- While inhaling, lift the chest above the ground and pull the legs towards the waist.
- Look ahead with a smile on your face.
- Remain steady in the posture, paying attention to your breathing, now your body is tight like a bow.
- Taking long deep breaths, relax in the asana.
- Be careful, do the asanas according to your capacity, do not tighten the body excessively.
- After 15-20 seconds, while exhaling, slowly bring the legs and chest back to the ground. Relax by releasing the esophagus.

Benefits of Dhanurasana

- To provide strength to the back/spine and abdominal muscles.
- To keep the genitals balanced.
- To relieve stiffness in chest, neck and shoulders.
- To strengthen the muscles of the hands and stomach.
- To make the spine flexible.
- Relief from stress and fatigue.
- Ease of constipation and menstruation.
- Regulation of kidney function.

Contraindications of Dhanurasana.

- If you have high or low blood pressure, hernia, back pain, headache, migraine (pain in one half of the head), neck injury/damage, or have recently had abdominal surgery, please do not try Dhanurasana.
- Pregnant women should not practice Dhanurasana.

7.2.2 Vakrasana Yoga

Vakrasana is an important asana among the asanas done while sitting. Vakrasana is derived from the word 'Vakra' which means crooked. In this asana, the spine is crooked or bent, that is why it is named Vakrasana. This asana increases the activity of the spine, protects you from diabetes, plays a very important role in depression, etc.

Method of doing Vakrasana Yoga

How to do this asana correctly, a simple method is being explained below, after understanding which you can easily do it at home.

- You sit on the ground with your legs spread.
- Make sure there is no distance between the two legs.
- Bend the left leg at the knee and lift it and place it next to the right knee.
- Keep the spine straight and while exhaling, turn the waist to the left.

- Now pull the knee of the left leg towards you with pressure using the elbow of the hand.
- You pull the leg towards you in such a way that there is pressure in the stomach. Maintain yoga as per your convenience.
- Exhale and come to the initial position.
- Repeat the same action from the other side.
- This is a cycle.
- In this way you do 3 to 5 cycles.

Figure-7.2: Method of doing Vakrasana

Breathing Process In Vakrasana

- While exhaling you turn to one side.
- Inhale slowly and exhale slowly.
- Take a long breath and come to the starting position.

Benefits of Vakrasana

- **Prevent Diabetes:** Vakrasana Yoga: Vakrasana is an excellent yoga practice to prevent diabetes. It activates the pancreas and helps in secretion of insulin in the right amount. In this way it plays an important role in the control and management of diabetes.
- **Vakrasana Yoga for weight loss:** By regular practice of this yoga you can reduce your belly fat. When this yoga

exercise is practiced, there is a good pressure in the stomach. By maintaining this yoga pose for a long time, the belly fat gradually starts melting. Not only this, you can also get relief from other stomach problems.

- **Panacea for the spine:** This yoga practice is a panacea for the spine. It has a huge contribution in making the spine healthy by making it flexible.
- **Vakrasana relieves back pain:** It reduces the spasm in your waist, makes it flexible and relieves you from back pain.
- **Protection from cramps and twists:** It protects you from cramps and twists of the spine.
- **Vakrasana to reduce depression:** With its regular practice you can overcome depression.
- **Best asana for the nervous system:** This makes the tantric system healthy and brings agility in its functioning.
- **Vakrasana to reduce constipation:** Practice of Vakrasana yoga revives the digestive system in a way which protects you from the problems of constipation, indigestion and gas.
- **Vakrasana for digestion:** This activates the stomach and all the organs related to digestion and proves helpful in the secretion of enzymes and hormones.
- **Vakrasana for lungs:** This increases lung capacity and is helpful in reducing most of the lung related problems.
- **Vakrasana for neck pain:** With its practice, the neck is also rotated to the right and left due to which the neck muscles gradually start loosening.

Precautions for Vakrasana

- Vakrasana should not be done in stomach pain.
- In case of knee pain, one should avoid doing this asana.
- Do not do this in case of severe back pain.
- One should avoid doing this if there is pain in the elbow.
- Avoid doing this even if you have neck pain.

7.2.3 Halasana

This asana is called Halasana because in its final posture the body looks like an Indian plough. If this yoga practice is done properly then it can prove to be very beneficial from health point of view. This asana is very beneficial for diabetes, thyroid etc. while reducing obesity. Since its shape looks like a plough, it is also called Plow Pose Yoga. Doing Halasana is not that easy. Those who cannot do this asana should do Ardhhalasana.

Figure-7.3: Method of doing Halasana

Method of Doing Halasana

Here the easy and simple method of Halasana has been explained. By understanding this, you can not only do this asana properly but can also get maximum benefit from it.

- Lie down on your back and keep your hands near the thighs.
- Now slowly without bending your legs, first raise them to 30 degrees, then to 60 degrees and then to 90 degrees.
- While exhaling, lift the back of the legs and take them behind the head and touch the toes with the ground.
- Now yoga posture has taken the form of Halasana.
- Inhale slowly and exhale slowly.
- Hold this asana as long as possible.
- Then slowly come back to the original position.
- This was a cycle.
- In this way you can do 3 to 5 cycles.

Benefits of Halasana

Halasana is a very important yoga practice in the world of asanas. Some of its benefits are being mentioned here:

- **To reduce belly fat:** By regular practice of this asana you can reduce your belly fat. And you can also control your weight.
- **To prevent hair fall:** By practicing this asana, blood flow increases in the head area and at the same time the hair starts getting the right amount of minerals. Which is good for hair health.
- **For facial beauty:** Daily practice of this makes your face glow.

- **For Thyroid:** This is a very suitable yoga exercise for thyroid and parathyroid gland. It controls metabolism and protects you from many problems by keeping your body weight under control.
- **Constipation:** It is beneficial in indigestion and constipation.
- **Diabetes:** It is very beneficial for diabetes.
- **Piles:** People who are suffering from piles should practice this asana.
- **Throat Disease:** It protects you from throat disorders.
- **Headache:** Those who suffer from headache should practice this yoga.

Contraindications of Halasana

- This asana should not be done by those who have cervical spondylitis.
- Avoid doing this if there is stiffness in the spine.
- This asana should not be done in high blood pressure.
- Do not perform this asana if you have back pain.
- Do not do this asana if you feel dizzy.
- Avoid doing this yoga during pregnancy and menopause.
- People suffering from heart disease should not do it.
- The maximum benefits of Halasana are obtained when Bhujangasana is done immediately after Halasana.

How to do Ardhahalasana

- Lie down on your back and keep your hands near the thighs.
- Now slowly without bending your legs, first raise them to 30 degrees, then to 60 degrees and then to 90 degrees.
- Maintain this position for some time.

- Then while exhaling, slowly bring the feet to the ground.
- This was a cycle.
- In this way you can do 3 to 5 cycles.
- Ardhahalasana is very beneficial in reducing your waist, indigestion, constipation, belly fat etc.

7.2.4 Ardhamatsyendrasana

Ardha – half, Matsyendra – king of fishes: Matsya – fish, Indra – king.

'Ardhamatsyendra' means to bend or rotate the body in half. Ardhamatsyendra asana is very beneficial for your spine. This asana helps in delivering the right amount of oxygen to the lungs or is very beneficial for the genitals. This asana is related to the spine, hence it should be done carefully.

Figure-7.4: Method of doing Ardhamatsyendrasana

Method of doing Ardhamatsyendrasana

- Sit with your legs extended in front, keep both the legs together, the spine should remain straight.
- Bend the left leg and place the heel of the left foot near the right hip (or you can also keep the left leg straight).
- Place the right foot in front over the left knee.
- Place the left hand on the right knee and keep the right hand behind.

- Look over the right shoulder by turning the waist, shoulders and neck to the right.
- The spine should remain straight.
- Maintain this position, keep taking long, deep normal breaths.
- While exhaling, first relax the right hand, then the waist, then the chest and finally the neck. Sit straight comfortably.
- Repeat the process from the other side.
- Exhale and come back to the front.

Benefits of Ardhamatsyendrasana

- The spine gets strengthened.
- Flexibility of the spine increases.
- By expanding the chest, the lungs get the right amount of oxygen.

7.2.5 Mandukasana

Mandukasana is a type of yoga asana and this asana is called Mandukasana because during this asana your position is exactly like that of a frog, that is, the position in which the frog is in, you also have the same position. Mandukasana is one such asana which can especially provide relief from diabetes and stomach problems like constipation, gas etc. But the question arises that what is Mandukasana, what is the method of Mandukasana i.e. how is it done and when should it be done, what are its benefits and so on. So let us know what is Mandukasana and why it is important to do it.

Method of doing Mandukasana

- To do Mandukasana, you should first sit on the cot or on the ground.
- Sit on the cot with your back straight. After this, bring both your knees together and bring your toes and heels near the buttocks.

- This posture of yours will be exactly like you sit in Vajrasana.
- After this, place the palms of both hands on top of each other and take them till the navel.
- Bend the upper part of the waist forward. Now your position will be such that your knees are on the ground, waist is upwards and legs are towards the back.

Now you have to take your chest till your thighs and remain in this position for some time.

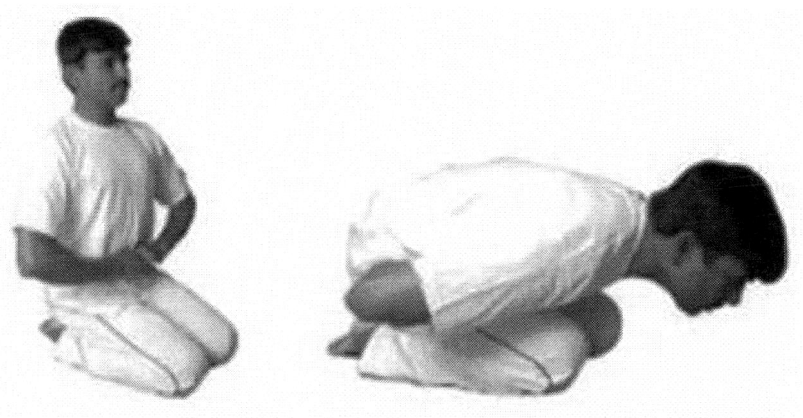

Figure-7.5: Method of doing Mandukasana

Benefits of Mandukasana

- The problem of gas produced in the stomach goes away.
- Other disorders like stomach problems can be easily cured.
- Spinal cord is strong.
- This asana strengthens your toes and increases your jumping ability, that is, you can jump comfortably for some time without getting tired.

- By doing this asana, the pancreas becomes effective in producing insulin and it is especially beneficial for the patients suffering from diabetes.
- Mandukasana is very beneficial in removing excess fat increasing in the body.
- Be it the problem of joint pain or pain in ankles, knees etc., all these problems can be easily relieved through this asana.

8.0
Yogic Practice and Benefits

8.1 Establishment of Vedic Science Centre, date (21 April 2015)

The Vedic Science Center was established by Shri Satish Kumar Singh, the founder School of Management Sciences and Chairman of the Group of Institutions, on Aakshya-Tritiya Vaishakh Shuklapaksha Day Tuesday Vikram Samvat 2072 dated 21 April 2015. Its main objective is to study the scientific researches underlying the mythological texts of India and to present them in the current modern by new avtar taking it to the public mind. The Indian system is being taught to unravel the secrets of life, by studying the spiritual lessons for keeping the body healthy through the scientific method of the mystery of yoga, with the new found researches, by students aimed at spreading the mantra of **"Vasudhaiva Kutumbakam"** in the world.

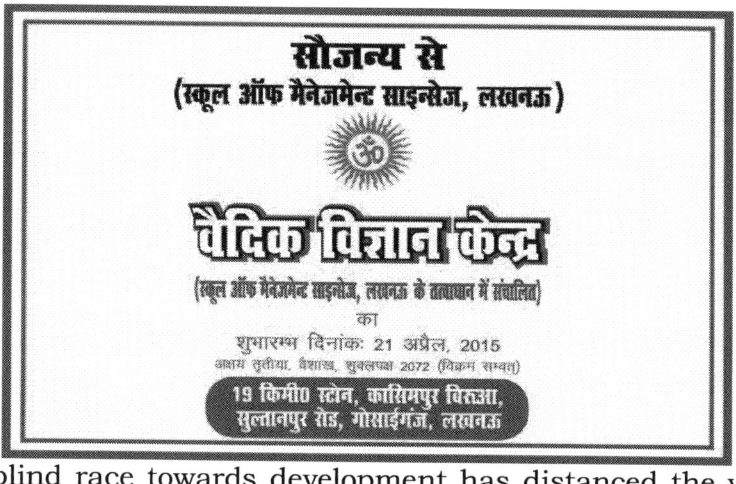

The blind race towards development has distanced the youth of India from its culture far away while the knowledge of 'Sanskrit language' has also been restricted to a few schools / institutions and universities. Today, there is a need to find out the role of Vedic Texts in industrial development. If these texts are beyond the perviews of present development yet part of it, is being bench marked, then technological development in 'Vedic Period' could have been more than what it is today.

Some facts found in recent times, make us rethink about the enthusiasm of the people of India that our ancestors who seems to be associated with religion were probably more scholarly and knowledgeable than we are now. There are things which have not been found and hence its research is necessary so that other countries could not tell us or teach us that the references in our ancient texts are correct.

Here, we would like to cite a few examples -

First: Goswami Tulsidas has written in the 'Hanuman Chalisa', few lines are -

“जुग सहस्र जोजन पर भानु।
लील्यो ताहि मधुर फल जानु।।”

“Jug Sahasra Jojan par Bhanu!
Lilyo Tahi Madhur Fal Janu!! ,

Today, when NASA has agreed with this research, we are accepting it as true.
Jug - Kaliyuga, Dwaaper, Treta and Satyuga. Its spans are 1200 years, 2400 years, 3600 years and 4800 years respectively; Total =12000 years.
Sahasra - 1000
Jojan - 8 miles and **Mile** - 1.6 km
Thus, distance from **Earth to Sun**: 12000 x 1000 x 8 x 1.6 = 15,36,00,000 km (15 crore 36 lakh km).

The lines of Hanuman Chalisa written by Goswami Tulsidas is now proving that in today's perspective, he was a great scholar of Astronomy or it was in the knowledge of all the people of that period.

Second: According to 'Ramcharitmanas' written by Goswami Tulsidas ji, Ram Setu was constructed under the supervision of Nal and Neel, civil engineering specialist according to the current language, to transport Sri Ram Chandra's entire army to Sri Lanka from India. It has been reported by NASA that this bridge was built by laying stones on the wood piling.

Also the stones used had less density and had the ability to float in water. The application of this principle by Nal-Neel is also confirmed in the Ramayana. The bridge is currently approximately 7 feet below the surface of water, which became possible due to increasing sea level over a period of 6,000 years.

NASA has named 'Sri Rameswaram Bridge' as Marvelous Civil Engineering of Vedic period.

Third: Our Vedic period inscriptions (Vedas and Puranas etc.) mention the sound of 'Om' in the Sun, which explains the Shankhanad of the word Omkar from time immemorial. Even today, there is a mention of awakening of Kundalini; it has been considered the path to enjoin soul with Brahma through meditation and through constant practice to connect with the Atmah.

Vision & Mission of Vedic Science Centre

Vision:

The Vedic wisdom of India, which was at the forefront of the world, has to be spread more and more to all scholars especially students studying in the technical field, as well as to open the pages of science and technology which have not been confirmed, by now their presence is large part of collective imagination.

Mission:

- Enhance in-depth study and knowledge of Vedic science.
- Study and spread the knowledge of Sanskrit language.
- Increase study and knowledge of Vedic-Mathematics.
- Simple benefits yoga's procedures.
- Meditation method and its benefits.
- Knowledge of the correct enounciation of 'Om' and the power derived from it.
- Knowledge of Kundalini and the method and benefits of awakening it.
- Remote communication with spirituality.
- Knowing about the activities of distant people through introversion.
- Communication of knowledge and science in the fetus in pregnancy.
- Knowledge of Aviation science and Science & Technology of all energies.
- Indepth knowledge about 'Yuga'.
- Knowledge of Indian calendar and astrology etc.
- Campaign to compile priceless texts related to spirituality.
- To advance welfare work in the public mind of the world with Vedic knowledge and science.
- To advance underlying knowledge from time to time.

8.2 Review Meeting of Vedic Science Center

After nearly a year, on 05.03.2016, a review meeting of the Vedic Science Center was convened under the chairmanship of Shri Gadadhar Narayan Sinha Retd. DG (Police), in which Shri Ram Shabda Mishra, Shri SBL Mehrotra, Shri Jagdish Chand Shah, Shri AC Mehrotra, Shri JB Singh and Shri Sharad Singh, Secretary and Executive Officer of SMS Institute, Director Prof. Bharat Raj Singh, Dr. Jagdish Singh, Dr. Dharmendra Singh etc., participated and the activities of the Vedic Science Center were discussed. Convenor Prof. Bharat Raj Singh apprised all the eminent thinkers about the treasure of wisdom in the ancient texts of India, it was found that many wonderful things are hidden in it and we should not get surprised to know that about 5000 years ago, the aircraft which was used by Shakuni Mama as mentioned in Mahabharata literature, is still available at Gandhar Hills in Afganistan. If this news is confirmed today, then it will not only make us proud but would be a testimony to our ancient literatures / texts written in Mahabharat, Ramayana, Vedas and Purans etc.

Prof. Singh also informed that the School of Management Sciences established 'Vedic Science Center' on 21 April 2015 last year, to discover the secrets hidden in the texts of India and to unfold it in respect of currently available technical knowledge. The basic mission of the center is to explore the knowledge available in the Vedas, Puranas, Mahabharata and Ramayana etc. and place it, before the scientific community of the state, country and abroad for future development in research field. The reports of valuable researches done under the Vedic Center in the last one year was read out and told that it has been disseminated to the students and teachers too. The report was reproduced as follows:

1) In order to advance human life in the structure of human body, blood is transmitted through the heart by the cells to every part of the body. In an occasional meeting with the enlightened class in and around Lucknow, it was ascertain that there is an iron content in the blood and the circulation of iron-bound blood through the arteries is being sustained. If any magnetic power is brought down from a scientific point of view, then electric energy will flow in the iron-bound blood running in the arteries. The body can experience an energy from which the power is transmitted with the help of consumption of external substances (food), this energy can be produced without any food or less food. This fact can be collaborated through the pronunciation of Vedic Mantras. Due to this, daily prayers have been started by the students and teachers and a different energy is being communicated to all the people and concentration on them has been increased in their studies as well.

2) At least one quarterly meeting of the Vedic Science Center has also been organized in which, while sharing the experiences of the enlightened class among themselves, it has also been decided to organize a one-hour yoga program on weekends, so that the students Mental and physical development can be accelerated among boys & girls. This program was started by some teacher on the last 'World-Yoga Day' (21 June 2015). According to their experience, it has been concluded that due to the vibrations of the breath that arise from the sclerosis, cranial and anterolateral, the strength of the arteries increases, and the blocked blood clots in the arteries also disappear.

3) In the old texts (Vedas-Puranas, Mahabharata and Ramayana etc.), there is also mention of aircraft or flying Khatole. For this also, this center is engaged in the search of the texts of India and the manuscript of the relics of the Aeronautical Scriptures, which was received by Maharishi Bharadhaj in India, was prepared in 1916 by Pandit Subarai Shastri. In which only six chapters were received. It was translated into English in the year 1973 by Ziyad Joshere. This center is also doing intensive study from time to time and information is provided about development in the field of mythology among students.

4) It has been informed by this center in the month of June 2015 that the aircraft used in Mahabharata, five thousand years ago, is located in a cave in the mountains of Afghanistan, which was brought to light by eight - American military commandos. An attempt was made to evacuate and due to unlimited energy in it, the eight commandos disappeared and till today they have not been detected. Not only this, the site inspection of the said aircraft was done by US President Barack Obama during his secret visit to Afghanistan and he also invited three Heads of State to see in January 2013, in which France, Germany, UK had visited. It is learned that the aircraft has since been taken up by the US NASA for research at the Douglas

Center. This information was posted on the US website Ancient Alien Disclose.tv from the revelation of American soldiers, the video of which has since been removed, but the audio of their soldiers' conversations is still available. The detailed video of the said video has been aired in February 2016 by IBN07.

At the end of the meeting, passing a vote of thanks to the Chairman Shri Gadadhar Narayan Sinha, it has been requested that all the enlightened-class, educationist and scientists of the state and India who are associated with this center, can share the scientific facts underline in the mythological texts of India. Help to bring the country to the forefront by reviving the heritage of unlimited knowledge associated with this land of India and by doing new research in the field of science and technology.

8.3 International Yoga Day, dated 21 June 2016

Director General of School of Management Sciences, Lucknow, Dr. Bharat Raj Singh has been imparting yoga training on International Yoga Day, by organizing a yoga camp in the college campus and spreading awareness about yoga among teachers, staff and students.

IV । दैनिक जागरण

जागरण सिटी

स्कूल ऑफ मैनेजमेंट साइंसेज द्वारा स्थापित वैदिक विज्ञान केंद्र में अंतरराष्ट्रीय योग दिवस पर शिक्षकों, कर्मचारियों व विद्यार्थियों को डॉ. भरत राज सिंह, आरएस मिश्रा और जीएन सिन्हा ने योग कराया।

योग का जलवा

हिन्दुस्तान 13

जनकल्याण समिति के तत्वाधान में नवनिर्मित विरामखण्ड-5 योगकेन्द्र में बारिश के बावजूद बड़ी संख्या में लोग शामिल हुए। योग की शक्ति के बारे में पर्यावरण वैज्ञानिक प्रो. भरत राज सिंह, कोआपरेटिव बैंक के सेवानिवृत जनरल मैनेजर आरएस मिश्रा व सेवानिवृत डीजीपी जीएन सिन्हा ने विस्तार से जानकारी दी। उधर, स्कूल ऑफ मैनेजमेण्ट साईसेंज में योग शिविर का आयोजन किया गया। जिसमें बड़ी संख्या में गणमान्य व्यक्तियों के साथ शिक्षकों, कर्मचारियों और कॉलेज के विद्यार्थियों ने हिस्सा लिया।

8.4 Inspection of NAAC Team-2017

In the year 2017, the School of Management Sciences, Lucknow was inspected by the NAAC (NAAC) and the annual results of the students from the team members appreciated the inclusion of daily prayer and yoga practice in the course schedule. The pre-eminent growth rate of 20-30% was also appreciated and also mentioned in NAAC's report.

8.5 International Yoga Camp in Sydney, Australia (dated 06 June-11 August 2018)

Today most of the people of the world have accepted that yoga fills the mind with peace, positive thinking and health of the body as well as abundant energy. It is also found from the data of the whole world that in countries where yoga is being adopted, there is reduction of about 40-60% in their medical bills of the people. Yoga is a legacy of our Bharatvarsha, which Rishis and Munis have provided 5000 years ago through their texts (Patanjali Yoga).

In a unique initiative by the Prime Minister of India, Narendra Modi, the idea of celebrating International Yoga Day was contemplated and in his speech delivered at UNGA on 27 September 2014, it was mentioned that "Yoga is an invaluable gift of India's ancient tradition. This symbolizes the concentration of mind and bodies. Yoga teaches the human mind to think, work, practice restraint, create harmony between man and nature. " Subsequently, on 11 December 2014, India's permanent representative Ashok Mukherjee prepared a proposal for it. 177 countries agreed to this draft and on 21 June 2015, the first International Day of Yoga was launched.

In the same sequence, Director General of School of Management Sciences, Lucknow, Dr. Bharat Raj Singh, gave yoga training at the international level by organizing a yoga camp at Aborn Park, Sydney (Australia) for one month and on World Yoga Day on 21 June 2018 Initiated to spread awareness about Yoga among the people and also greeted people on Yoga Day.

8.6 Inspection of NAAC Team-2023

During the year 2023, the School of Management Sciences, Lucknow was inspected by the National Assessment and Accreditation Council (NAAC) peer team and the results of the students were found above 90% by the inclusion of daily prayer and yoga practice in the course schedule. The peer team appreciated the intiative and also mentioned in NAAC's report. SMS graded A+ during 2nd cycle.

8.7 Experinces / Opinions of Regular Yoga Practiceners

i). Gorakh Prasad Nishad (16 October 2020)

I have crossed 82 years of age. I used to have difficulty in walking and pain in joints. I got this condition at the age of about 70 years because my blood pressure suddenly increased on a day and due to that my left side of the body was paralysed. Since, a yoga center was being run by Dr. Bharat

Raj Singh and Shri Ram Shabda Mishra in Vasanti-Park near my house, in which yogic practice / training was being conducted regularly since 2012, I started attending yoga classes since 2015 and practicising regular Praanyama, Bhramari and Udgith along with Bhastika, Kapala-Bhati and Anulom-Antonyms. I have now got rid of the pain of joints and a relief in prostate enlargement.

I therefore advise everyone to do regular yogic activities and make their life happy.

Gorakh Prasad Nishad,
Former Minister, Animal Husbandry,
Viram Khand- 5/850, Gomtinagar, Lucknow.

ii). Mukesh Kumar Singh (31 October 2020)

I am about 49 years old. I used to regularly read the articles related to yoga published by Dr. Bharat Raj Singh in the "Science & Health" column of news papers and magazines and decided to start yoga practice. Since I attained my weight 110 kg in the year 2016, I started attending regular Yoga practice conducted at the Janeshwar Park, Lucknow and after 10-12 months my weight came down to 85 kg and new glow was created in the body. Due to the reduction of 25 kg in my weight during the year 2016 to 2017, I participated in many National Races and won second position in the 10 km race.

In the continuation to this, I took higher yoga classes and received the Post Graduate Diploma Certificate in Yoga.

Now I am conducting regular yoga classes as a Yoga Trainer and also making people aware about the yogic consciousness towards alignment of mind, heart and health to the public at large.

Mukesh Kumar Singh,
Yoga Instructor
Doordarshan Accounting Department,
Lucknow.

iii). Dr. Bharat Raj Singh (15 November 2020)

I have crossed 77 years of my age. Since 2009, I started feeling complaint of urine retensation (i.e., prostate enlargement). On the advice of doctors, tests were carried out in the labs of various hospitals and the situation of increase in uric-acid was informed. A test in SPGI, Lucknow showed that it could affect the kidneys. Then I took advise of a doctor situated at Aliganj who informed me that my prostate was enlarged and need to be operated with a laser, otherwise the problem could further worsen.

In the test report, my urine-retensation was found over 35 grams and temporarily the doctor adviced me to start taking Urimax-30 capsule daily for immediate relief, but after a few days, the side effects of the medicine was noticed and I suffered with stomach upset, which forced me to stop the use of this drug. Since I was doing regular yoga, I started Kapalabhati for more than 20 to 30 minutes and regular external Praanyama and mandook Praanyam, my prostate complaint was found negligible after few months and now during past 10-11 years, I am living a normal life without any treatment.

On my own experiences, I suggest to the public that you must do yoga practice regularly to make life happier, and also will feel increasing concentration of your mind and become a participant for the the development of your nation with new zeal.

Dr. Bharat Raj Singh,
Environmentalist and
Director General (Technical),
School of Management Sciences,
Lucknow.

iv). Shri Rajeev Bhatia (15 April 2022)

I am about 55 year's old and doing yoga regularly even after being posted in Bank of India, Mumbai for a long period. After joining Bank of India, Regional Office, Vibhuti Khand, Lucknow, from January 2020, I am came in contact with Prof. Bharat Raj Singh. Since I was suffering from prostate problem, one day I shared my problem with Dr. Singh. He advised me todo yoga 20 to 30 minutes regularly with a combination of Kapal Bhati Praanyama, Titli Asana and Manduk-Asana and asked me to report the progress after two-weeks. It felt like a miracle as the frequency of urination which was 3-4 times in the night reduced to 1-2 and I also stopped my Uri-Max medicine.

I have fully recovered now and feel great. I thank Dr. Bharat Raj Singh, in-charge of the Center for Yoga and Vedic Science, who gave me new light about the treatment of many diseases through regular yoga practice.

Rajeev Bhatia,
Branch Manager, Bank of India, Regional Office,
Vibhuti Khand, Gomti Nagar, Lucknow.

v). Shri Umesh Chand Tiwari (05 May 2022)

I am about 68 years old, retired IAS from UP Govt. and living at Viram Khand-5 /51, Gomti Nagar, Lucknow. During my service period, I had developed a habit of smoking cigarettes continuously. Although I met Dr. Bharat Raj Singh when I was in the Public Works Department; but we were in regular touch at the Yoga Center, Vasanti Park since 2016. He suggested me to sit for half an hour under the Peepal tree in the park; take oxygen and start watering to plants and trees. This has given meraculus relief to break my habit of smoking cigarettes and I feel better now. Today I encourage people to do yoga regularly.

Umesh Chand Tiwari,
IAS (Retd.), 5/51, Viram Khand,
Gomti Nagar, Lucknow.

vi).Shri Ramayan Singh (15 July 2022)

I am about 83 years old, retired from Pradeshik Armed Constabulary (PAC) as Head Clerk and living in Viram Khand-5, Gomti Nagar. I met Dr. Bharat Raj Singh during morning walk since 2008. We continue to meet at the Yoga Center, Vasanti Park and take walk and do some postures of yoga. I am suffering from Piles (Fistula) deseases. He suggested me to practice meditation and yoga daily and to eat fresh and light hot food to get rid of fistula. Today I am in great relief by doing regular meditation and yoga and also by changing my food habits.

Ramayan Singh,
5/611, Viram Khand,
Gomti Nagar, Lucknow

vii).Shri SBL Mehrotra (10 February 2023)

I'm approximately 78 years old. I completed my Mechanical Engineering degree from SVNIT, Surat in 1970. I retired from Uttar Pradesh Agro Ltd. and currently reside at Viram Khand-5/521, Gomtinagar, Lucknow. I used to experience discomfort in my lower back and leg joints while walking.

Dr. Bharat Raj Singh, who was a year junior to me in college, follows a daily yoga practices at the Yoga Centre in Vasanti Park. Since adopting his yoga practices, I've noticed a significant improvement in my well-being. I now encourage my peers and friends to prioritize regular yoga practice for their overall health and wellness.

SBL Mehrotra,
5/521, Viram Khand, Gomti Nagar,
Lucknow.

Reference

1. **Pranic Healing** - Master Chao Kak Sui
2. **Realization of the Spirit by Meditation** - Master Chao Kak Sui
3. **The Spiritual Essence of Man** - Master Chao Kak Sui
4. **Rigveda-**Yogic Actions
5. **Patanjali Yoga**
6. **Hatha Pradipika**
7. **Gherand Code**
8. **ViGyaan Bhairav Tantra**
9. **Pradipika Granth**
10. **Yoga Compilation** – Swami Ram Dev
11. **Yoga Darshan** –Sri Sri Ravi Shankar
12. **Raja Yoga Discourse Series**
13. **True Yogi Life**
14. **Raja Yoga in Home Life**
15. **True Peace of Mind**
16. **Gyaan Yoga Pathway**
17. **Method and Siddhi of Yoga**
18. **Life with Sattvik Yoga**
19. **Yoga Darshan (Hindi)** - Dr. Bharat Raj Singh
20. **Yoga Philosphy** - Dr. Bharat Raj Singh
21. **Superbrain Yoga and Dhyan (Hindi)**-Dr. Bharat Raj Singh

22. Superbrain Yoga and Meditation (Eng) - Dr. Bharat Raj Singh

23. Pranic Urja (Hindi) – Dr. Bharat Raj Singh

24. Pranic Energy (Eng) – Dr. Bharat Raj Singh

25. Yoga Vigyan (Hindi)– Dr. Bharat Raj Singh

Index

Publisher:

Lulu Press Inc.

627, Davis Drive, Suite 300, Morrisville, NC 27560, USA

Printed in Dunstable, United Kingdom

80335477R00100